Philena's Friendship Quilt

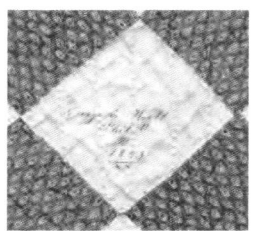

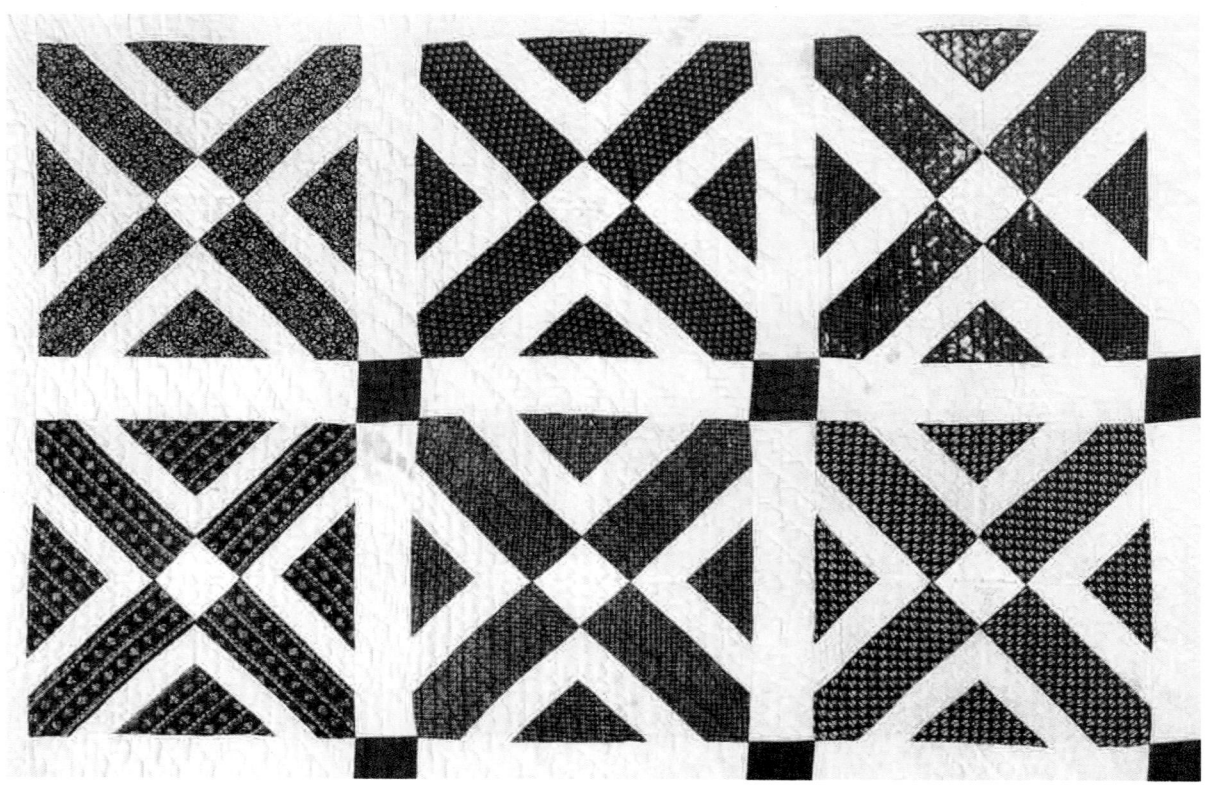

The Ohio Quilt Series

Ricky Clark, Ellice Ronsheim, and Donna Sue Groves, series editors

Quilts of the Ohio Western Reserve, by Ricky Clark

Uncommon Threads: Ohio's Art Quilt Revolution, by Gayle A. Pritchard

Album Quilts of Ohio's Miami Valley, by Sue C. Cummings

Philena's Friendship Quilt: A Quaker Farewell to Ohio, by Lynda Salter Chenoweth

Philena's Friendship Quilt

A Quaker Farewell to Ohio

LYNDA SALTER CHENOWETH

Ohio University Press

ATHENS

Ohio University Press, Athens, Ohio 45701
www.ohioswallow.com
© 2009 by Ohio University Press
All rights reserved

To obtain permission to quote, reprint, or otherwise reproduce
or distribute material from Ohio University Press publications,
please contact our rights and permissions department at
(740) 593–1154 or (740) 593–4536 (fax).

Printed in China
Ohio University Press books are printed on acid-free paper ⊗ ™

16 15 14 13 12 11 10 09   5 4 3 2 1

Library of Congress Cataloging-in-Publication Data
Chenoweth, Lynda Salter, 1941–
    Philena's friendship quilt : a Quaker farewell to Ohio / by
Lynda Salter Chenoweth.
        p. cm. — (Ohio quilt series)
    Inclues bibliographical references and index.
    ISBN 978-0-8214-1858-1 (pb : alk. paper)
    1. Quaker quilts—Ohio. 2. Signature quilts—Ohio. 3. Friendship
quilts—Ohio. 4. Hambleton, Philena Cooper, 1822–1915. I. Title.
    NK9198.H36C48 2009
    746.4609771—dc22
                            2009000023

For Nellie, whom I miss.

It is a hard thing to bear, this separation from those we love while yet on earth. Those that have passed away from all the cares and sorrows of life, however dear they were, we *know* they cannot *return*. They are blest and we give them up. But for those that are still subjected to all the vicissitudes of this ever-changing scene, how many anxious fears will arise, with the faint hopes of meeting once again.

Anna Briggs Bentley
12th mo 20th 1827
Columbiana County

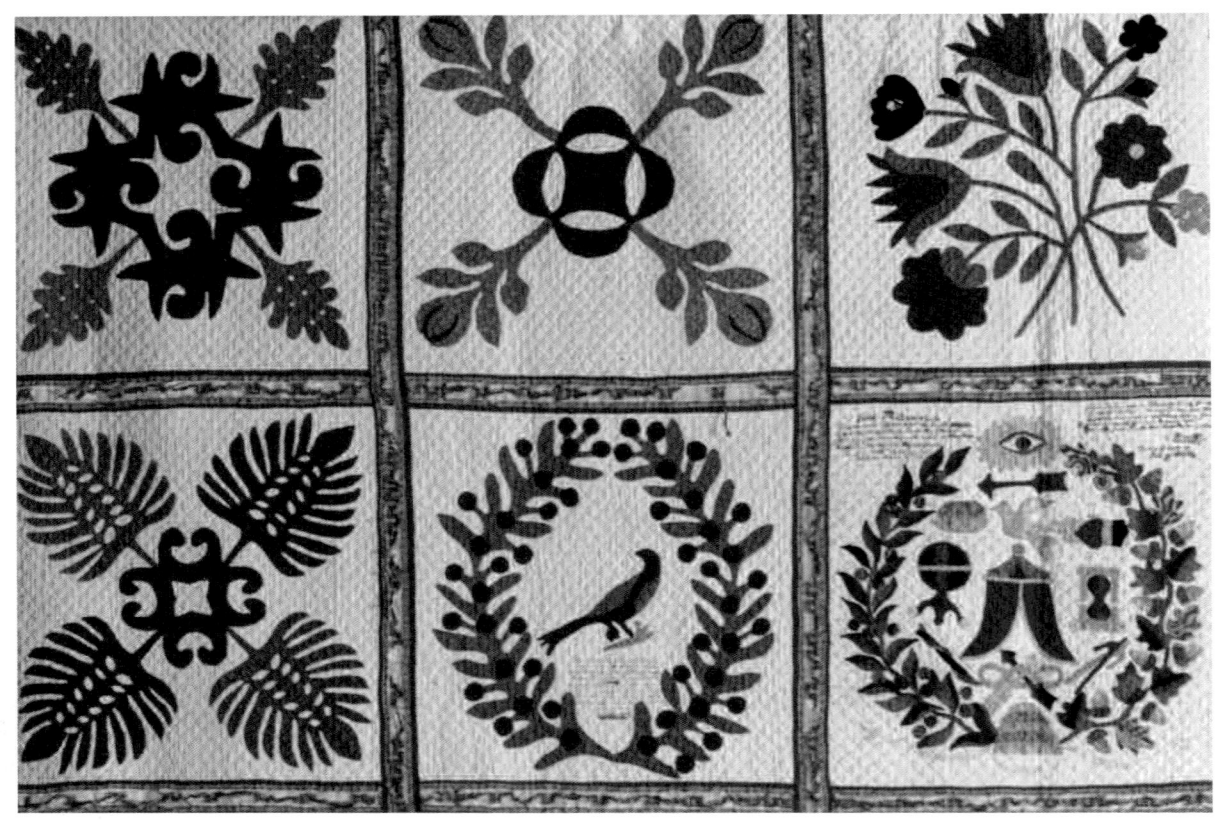

Contents

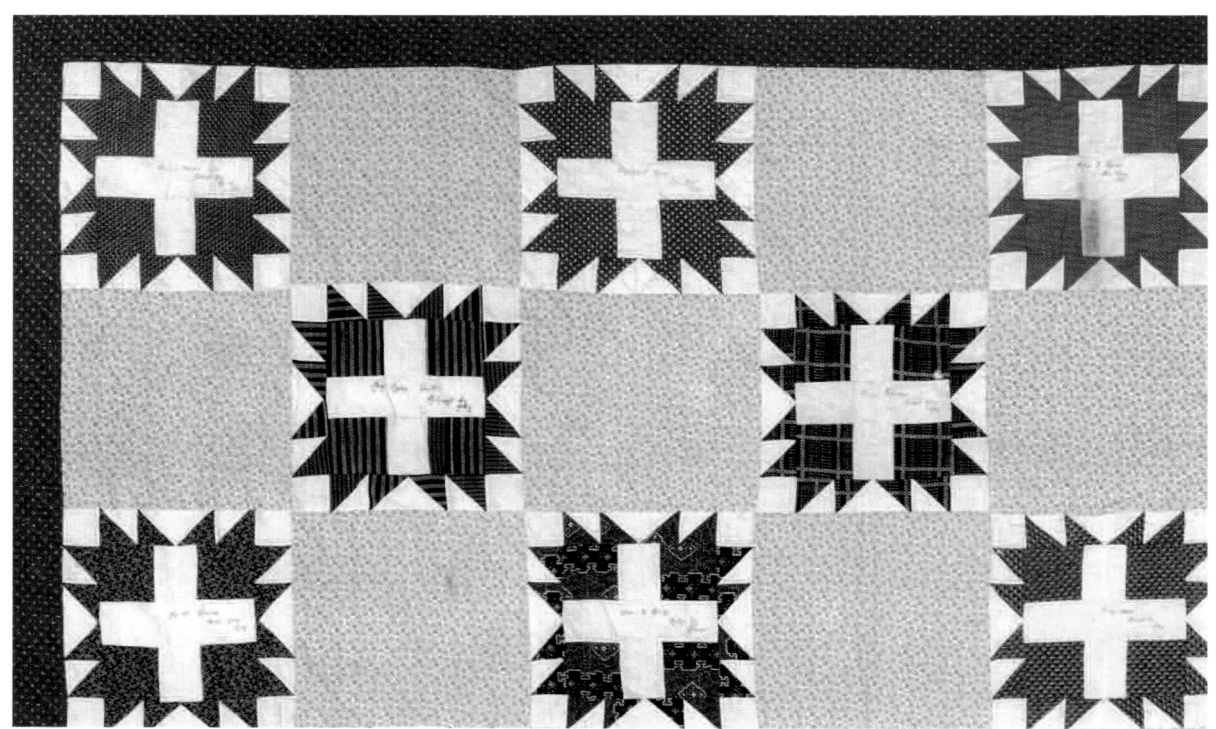

Illustrations

Acknowledgments

MANY PEOPLE ACROSS THE COUNTRY CON-
tributed their time and effort to discover the identity of Philena Cooper Hambleton and reveal the
community of people whose names are inscribed on
her quilt.

Foremost, I owe a huge debt of gratitude to Tina
Frantz, a resident of Salem, Ohio, and the editor of
The Columbiana County Connection published by
the Ohio Genealogical Society. Tina's sleuthing in
county and regional records provided a wealth of
primary source documents and her knowledge of
the history and geography of Columbiana County,
Ohio, was invaluable. Second, I thank George
Zeller and his cousin Helen Ward Wolfgang for
their contributions to my research. Thanks are also
given to Lenore Sechler, president of the Hanover
Township Historical Society, who provided guidance and documents from the society that helped
immensely.

In Iowa, I thank Pat Rowell, a volunteer researcher at the Poweshiek County Historical and
Genealogical Society, who located the Hambleton
graves at the Lynnville Friends Cemetery and provided important historical information from local
sources. Also in Iowa, Gary D. Craver of Centerville helped solve the mystery of how Philena's quilt
made its way to California. Joyce Hambleton
Whitten, in Arkansas, gave me genealogical information about the Hambleton family that enabled
me to pursue their stories and that of Philena.

Michele DeParasis, in Massachusetts, generously
provided family information that explained the
origins and identity of Philena's mother, Rachel
Bonner Erskine Cooper. In Pennsylvania, I extend
particular thanks to James Hazard, a volunteer researcher at the Friends Historical Library of
Swarthmore College, who retrieved and copied
early Quaker records to provide me with documents and information I would not have been able
to obtain otherwise.

My thanks also go to Dawn Moser in El Cerrito,
California, whose editorial advice and knowledge of
quilting techniques, fabric, and American history
contributed greatly to this effort; to Joyce Gross,
who gave me unlimited access to her extensive
quilt history archives in Petaluma, California; to
Beth Donaldson at the Michigan State University
Museum, who prepared the instructions and dia-
grams for reproducing Philena's quilt; to David
Stratton at the Salem Historical Society in Salem,
Ohio, who found and copied relevant materials; to
Kenneth Kline, who welcomed us to his house and
property in Butler Township, Columbiana County;
and to Tassy Aldridge Guthrie, who graciously let
us visit her home in Searsboro, Iowa, where Philena
lived after she moved to Iowa.

I extend special thanks to quilt historians Ricky
Clark and Marsha MacDowell for reading the origi-
nal manuscript, and to Ricky, Donna Sue Groves,
Ellice Ronsheim, and Gillian Berchowitz at Ohio

University Press for their editorial assistance. Special thanks also to Philena's descendants Jerome, Lora, and Katie Walker of Los Angeles for the use of their photographs of Philena and other family members and for generously sharing details of their family history. Finally, loving thanks to my husband, Theodore H. Chenoweth, who never failed to encourage this effort, provided unlimited help editorially, and accompanied me to Ohio and Iowa in search of Philena and those named on her quilt.

Philena's Friendship Quilt

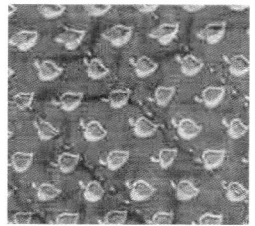

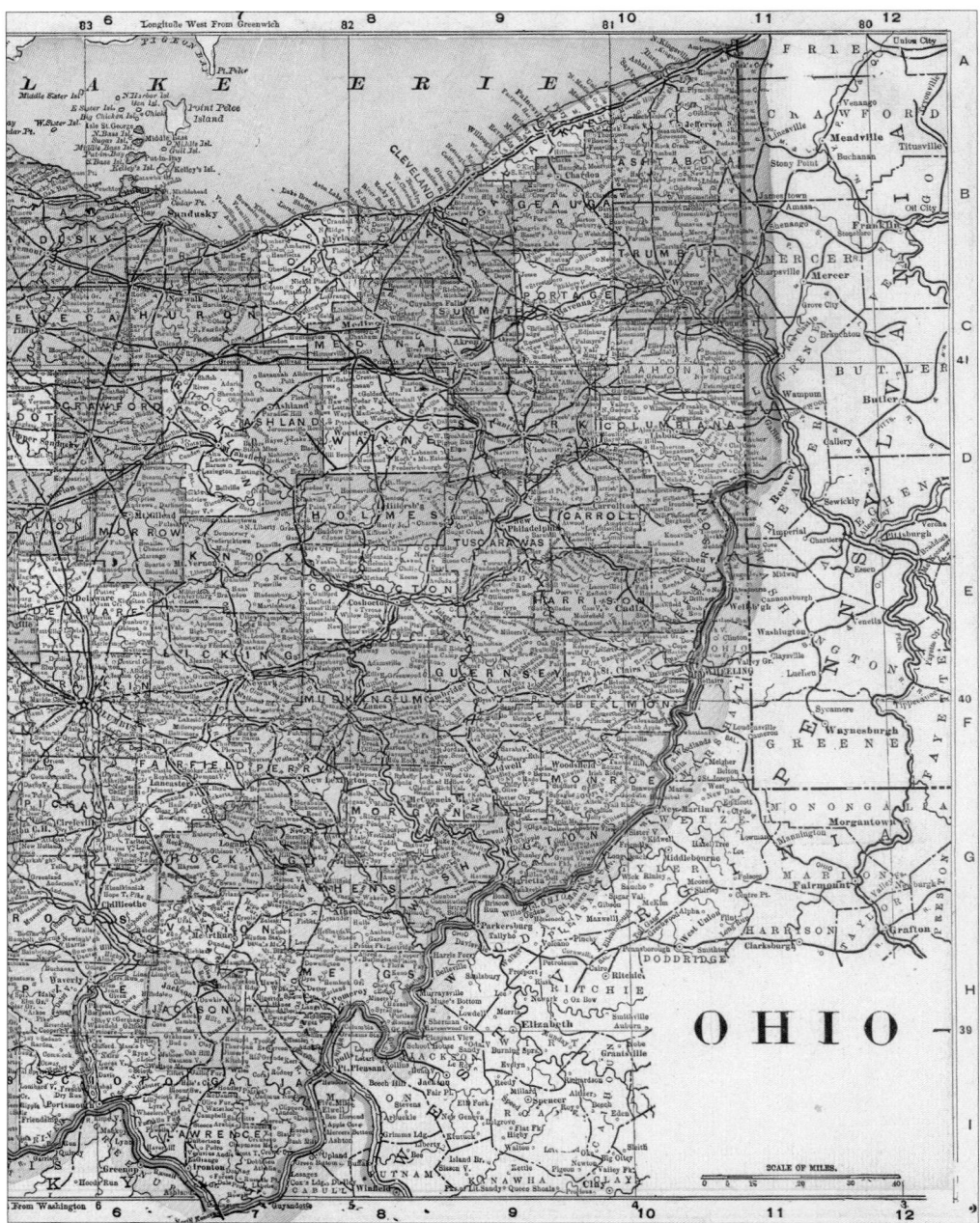

ILLUSTRATION 1. Map of northeastern Ohio showing the location of Columbiana County, the fourth county south of Lake Erie on the Pennsylvania border. From a page of *Cram's Universal Atlas: Geographical, Astronomical and Historical* (George F. Cram, 1898).

Introduction

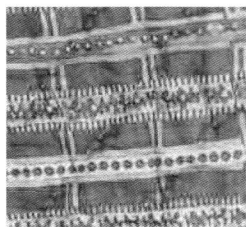

LATE ONE AFTERNOON IN AUGUST 2001, MY husband and I attended the last day of the annual Petaluma Quilt Show on the Petaluma River in northern California. This show provides an opportunity for local quilters to display and have judged what they have made during the prior year. Even though I make quilts and enjoy looking at new ones, what draws me to this show each year is my interest in antique quilts and their individual fabrics. Petaluma's merchants take advantage of the popularity of the show to stock antique bedding and linen during the event.

Ted and I wandered in and out of several shops in search of nineteenth-century quilts and fabric. It was getting late and businesses would soon close. I had not seen anything older than about 1910 and was getting discouraged. Just one more antique store . . .

I was getting ready to leave this last shop when I spotted, in the farthest back corner, an old shelf unit with glass doors. On the very bottom shelf, wadded up almost out of sight, I caught a glimpse of nineteenth-century fabrics. I pulled out the quilt,

sat down on a bench nearby, and began to examine it. At first I didn't see the writing. It was badly faded, but there were names written on each of the quilt's twenty-five blocks. On closer scrutiny, I saw that the date 1853 appeared on most of them.

I had found a signature quilt displaying the names of family and friends—a record of cherished relationships that existed in 1853. We bought the quilt and took it home. Thus began my search to identify the woman for whom the quilt was made and understand her relationship to those named on her quilt. It was the first step on a path that would eventually lead me twice to Columbiana County, Ohio, and once to Poweshiek County, Iowa.

Before leaving the store, I asked the cashier to call the dealer who was selling the quilt and ask her where she had gotten it. The dealer would not disclose the source of the quilt but did say that the quilt "had always been in the family and had come from an estate in Oklahoma."

Close examination of the quilt at home slowly revealed the names and other information that had been written on the quilt blocks in black ink. I say "slowly" because the writing was so faint that I had to scrutinize it in various kinds of light, including fluorescent and ultraviolet, and at different times of day, to make out the names. Surprisingly, the most effective light was in the morning when there was heavy fog from Bodega Bay flowing down the hills to the west and hanging over the town of Sonoma where I live.

The two main families on the quilt appeared to be the Hambletons and the Coopers. Most of the blocks listed New Garden as the town, Columbiana County as the county, Ohio as the state, and, in almost all cases, 1853 as the year.

With this information to guide me, I began searching for Coopers and Hambletons on Internet genealogical sites and Web sites sponsored by historical societies in Ohio and in other states mentioned on the quilt. Hours at the computer produced no information about the Cooper family and only a bit of information about the Hambletons.

I was making little progress until I came across an Internet Message Board where David Eyre, who happened to live in Germany, had posted some information about Joel G. Hambleton, one of the men named on the quilt. I sent him an email about my quilt, and he forwarded my message to his cousin Joyce Hambleton Whitten in Arkansas. Within a day, I received an email from Joyce with an attachment detailing the descendants of John Hambleton, head of the branch of the family that migrated to Ohio from Pennsylvania in the early nineteenth century. Not only did I now have information about specific Hambletons whose names appeared on the quilt, I also learned that they were Quakers, members of the Religious Society of Friends.

The Religious Society of Friends was founded in England by George Fox in the mid-seventeenth century. Nineteenth-century Quakers were distinguished by their belief that no priest or clergyman, no "temple" or church, and no formal rites were needed to establish communion with God. Rather, they relied on the "Inner Light" instilled in all hearts by the Holy Spirit to understand and guide them in the Divine Truth. They adhered to a strict Christian life, generally refused to bear arms against other human beings, believed in the equality of all men and women, abhorred slavery and capital punishment, and promoted education and philanthropy to better the lives of others. Further, they closely monitored the behavior and movements of their members, keeping detailed records that proved invaluable to my research into the Hambletons and other families named on the quilt.

As time went by, I realized that I needed to go to Columbiana County in search of Quaker and other records that might reveal more about the lives of the people named on the quilt. The basic information I was collecting from Internet sources, such as census data or listings of marriage and death dates, did not reveal the personal aspects of life needed to understand the experiences and interrelationships of the community I had begun to think of as my own.

We arrived in Columbiana County in the fall of 2002. There I contacted Tina Frantz, a genealogical researcher and the editor of *The Columbiana County Connection*, published by the Columbiana County Chapter of the Ohio Genealogical Society. She directed me to the historical and genealogical resources in the Salem Library in Perry Township. Here I later spent hours leafing through Hinshaw's

Encyclopedia of American Quaker Genealogy and local historical documents. From Hinshaw I learned that "my" Hambletons had been disowned for becoming Hicksites, a group that separated from the Orthodox Quakers during a schism that occurred in the late 1820s. There the trail ended.

Tina then suggested that we visit the Hanover Township Historical Society in Hanoverton to see if they had the Hicksite records for the New Garden Monthly Meeting. New Garden was both a Friends meeting and the small town repeatedly mentioned on the quilt. Lenore Sechler, president of the society, gave us access to the society's holdings, which included minutes that covered New Garden Anti-Slavery Society meetings for the years 1838, 1839, and 1840. These minutes mentioned three sought-after Hambletons, as well as other people named on the quilt. We also found "The Reminiscences of Edwin Dutton," a personal memoir that described life in the Hanover Township area in the early and mid-nineteenth century as well as the arrival, from Pennsylvania, of the Mendenhall family, whose names also appear on the quilt.

After our return to California, I began to pursue "the Iowa connection." Two of the couples were described on the quilt as living in Cedar County, Iowa. Also, Chalkley J. Hambleton, in his 1887 *Geneological [sic] Record of the Hambleton Family, Descendants of James Hambleton of Bucks County, Pennsylvania,* mentioned that members of the Hambleton family had moved from Ohio to Poweshiek County, Iowa, in the mid-nineteenth century.

I returned to the Internet, where I found a Web site for the Poweshiek County Historical and Genealogical Society and discovered Pat Rowell, a volunteer at the society who conducts research for people wanting information about the county's families and history. Through Pat's remarkable digging in old records, I received obituaries and articles about the county's early pioneers that revealed details of the lives of almost all of the Hambletons whose names appear on the quilt. Through other contacts, Pat and I also discovered where the Hambletons were buried.

My husband and I returned to Columbiana County with the quilt in 2004 to continue my research and to attend the Fiftieth Annual Reunion of the Ward family, whose ancestor, Peter Ward, is named on the quilt. Again, I got in touch with Tina Frantz and finally met her face-to-face. Together we discovered relevant graves not found before, gathered probate and other records that gave insight into the material and social life of people listed on the quilt, and, using property maps from 1841, 1860, and 1870, found the nineteenth-century homes of some of the people named on the quilt. These homes included the house where the Hambletons lived at the time the quilt was made.

The success of our stay in Ohio inspired us to go on to Iowa, where the Hambletons had moved when they left Columbiana County. We made reservations in the tiny town of Lynnville, where Pat Rowell had located the Hambleton tombstones. Our first destination was the Friends Cemetery to visit the graves of the Hambletons who are buried there. By this time, I knew the quilt had been made for Philena Cooper Hambleton, and I placed a bouquet of flowers on her grave.

The next day we traveled to Montezuma to visit the Poweshiek County Historical and Genealogical

Society. There we copied property maps, obituaries, short biographies of early pioneers, and information from business directories and other nineteenth-century sources. These materials enabled us to locate the land the Hambletons had purchased when they moved to Iowa, and to visit the home, now owned by Tassy Aldridge Guthrie, that Osborn and Philena Hambleton built in 1855.

While we were peering at Tassy's house from the edge of her yard, she spotted me and came outside to see what I was doing. I introduced myself and told her about Philena, the quilt, and our trip from Ohio to Iowa. Tassy recognized the Hambleton name as that of the first owner of her property and was astounded that I had appeared out of nowhere knowing the history of the couple who had first owned her home. As our conversation continued, she asked if I had the quilt with me. I said that I did, and she asked if she could see it. I retrieved the quilt from the trunk of our car and took it inside. We spread it out on the dining room table, where the glancing sun of a fall afternoon shone through the window. Standing there, seeing the quilt aglow on a table in what had once been Philena's parlor, I realized that Ted and I had traveled a path Philena had taken 149 years earlier. It was the second time the quilt had made this journey.

Signature Quilts

Family and Friends Stitched Together in Time

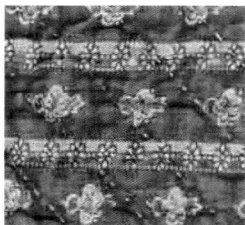

PHILENA'S QUILT WAS COMPLETED AND SIGNED in 1853. This was near the midpoint of a more-than-twenty-year period during which signature quilts experienced great popularity in America. They suddenly appeared at the beginning of the 1840s and peaked in popularity by the middle of the decade. Their appeal had begun to decline by the late 1850s,[1] but women continued to make signature quilts in large numbers into the 1870s. By the late 1870s, the deprivation caused by the Civil War had been replaced by prosperity across most of the country. With prosperity came a decline in the popularity of cotton signature quilts, and women began to apply their needlework to the latest fad—crazy quilts of silks, wools, and velvets, often ornamented with embroidery and applied decorations such as beads, ribbons, and lace.[2] Cotton signature quilts continued to be made after this time, especially in western states where new settlement was still taking place.[3] By the early 1900s, signature quilts were made to raise money for churches and charities.

ILLUSTRATION 2. Ink signature on a Christian Cross quilt, c. 1840–50. Maker unknown, upstate New York. 76½" × 92½". The Christian Cross pattern is also known as Chimney Sweep. The names of thirty women appear on this quilt, all inscribed by a single hand on separate blocks. The surnames represented are Starr, Wheeler, Pickering, Baker, Curtice, Bartlett, Tewiliger, Curtis, Hubbard, Drake, and Updike. The women are listed as being from Ithaca, Newfield, Auburn, and Enfield, New York. Cotton. Pieced, ink inscriptions. Author's collection.

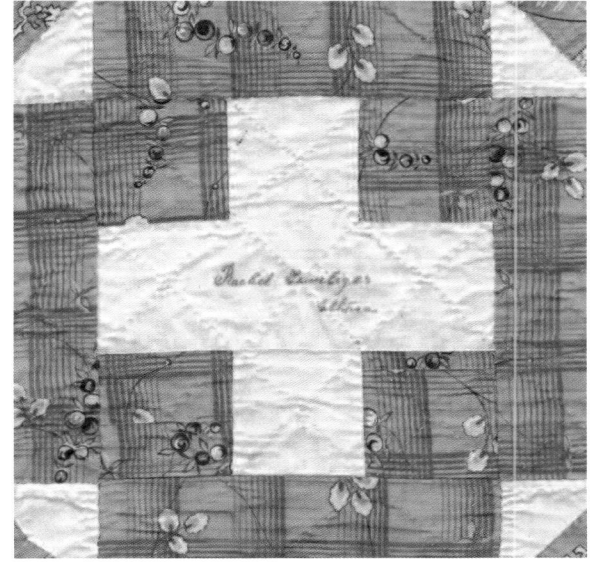

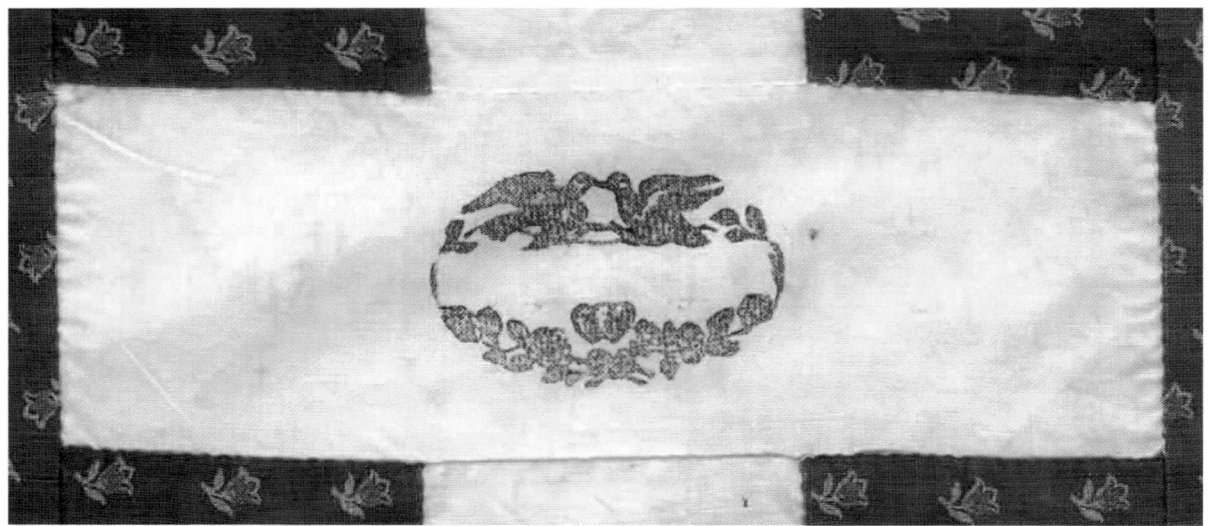

ILLUSTRATION 3. Example of the imprint of a metal stamp, first inked and then applied to the block for later signature within its decorative motif. These stamps came with a set of movable type that could be set within the stamp's rectangular opening. Photographs of metal stamps displaying exactly the same decorative motif as that shown on this stamped block can be seen in Sandi Fox, *For Purpose and Pleasure: Quilting Together in Nineteenth-Century America*, 31, and Jessica F. Nicoll, *Quilted for Friends: Delaware Valley Signature Quilts, 1840–1855*, 10. The stamp shown in Nicoll's book is a holding of the Chester County Historical Society (PA) and is dated c. 1840. The block pattern is Christian Cross. Author's collection.

The emergence of signature quilts in the 1840s paralleled the popularity of autograph albums at the time, as well as the increasing nineteenth-century perception of women as both custodians and documenters of family history and interrelationships.[4] Autograph albums had appeared in America by the 1820s,[5] but it was not until the 1830s and 1840s that they were widely used to document family ties and friendships, the latter frequently commemorated by verses taken from contemporary publications. One popular source for album verses in the 1830s, and then again in the 1840s when a renewed interest in these albums occurred, was *The Lady's Book*, later known as *Godey's Lady's Book and Magazine*. This publication had a formal circulation of 17,500 in 1840 that grew to 150,000 prior to the Civil War. These figures fail to reflect, however, the number of additional readers who received the publication as women passed their issues on to relatives and friends living nearby or moving west.[6]

Women in the 1840s soon transferred the popularity of the autograph album to another medium; that of the quilt. These new "albums" were inscribed with inks inconsistent in quality and colorfastness in spite of ongoing commercial efforts, which extended into the twentieth century, to produce an indelible black ink that would not fade or damage paper, cotton, and linen.[7] These inks

ILLUSTRATION 4. Typeset or stenciled name appearing on a signature quilt made about 1875 in Bethlehem, New Hampshire. The quilt, which measures 80" × 88", is made up of 116 Nine Patch Diamond blocks, each displaying either a handwritten, stamped, or stenciled name. A stencil that produced a decorative, floral swag was also used on this quilt. Author's collection.

were used to write on quilt blocks freehand with quill or steel pens, and also to imprint drawings, names, and verses by use of stencils and engraved stamps.[8] Two types of signature quilts became fabric "albums" at this time. These types are categorized by Barbara Brackman as the *sampler album quilt* and the *single-pattern friendship quilt*.[9] Both were made to document and commemorate family and community relationships and to mark significant life events.

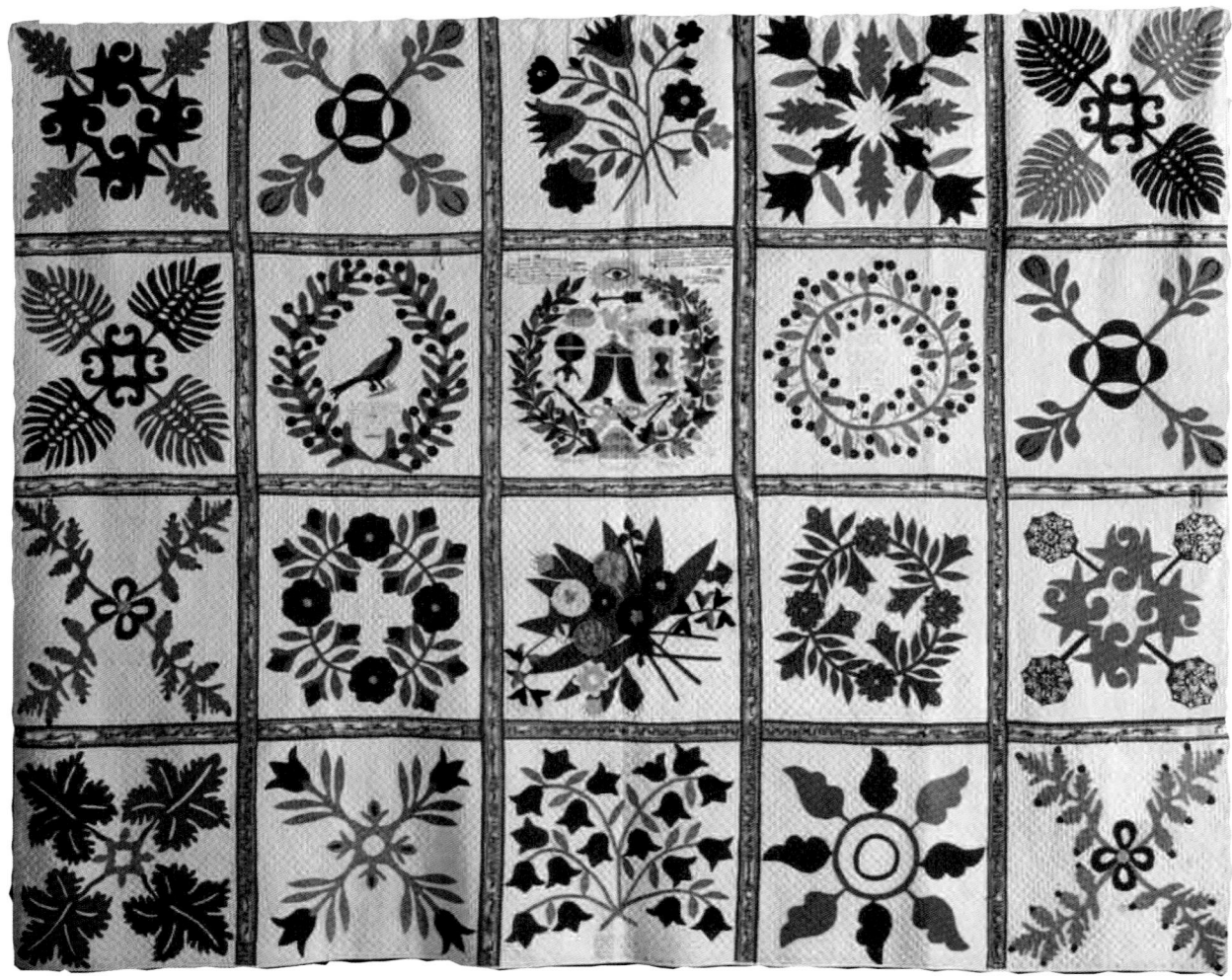

ILLUSTRATION 5. Sampler album quilt, c. 1849. Made by Lizetta Hicksecher, Canal Dover, Ohio. 71" × 79". The quilt is made up of appliquéd squares with poetry inscriptions; one block displays symbols of the International Order of Odd Fellowship, a fraternal organization. Cotton. Ink inscriptions. Collection of the Museum of History and Industry, Seattle, Washington.

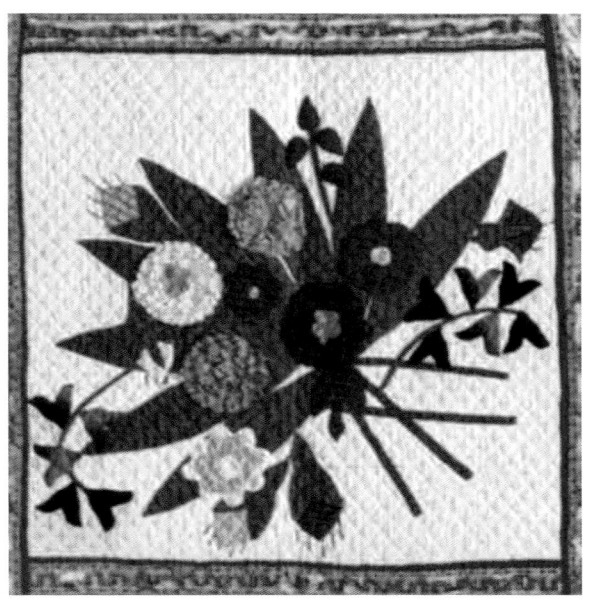
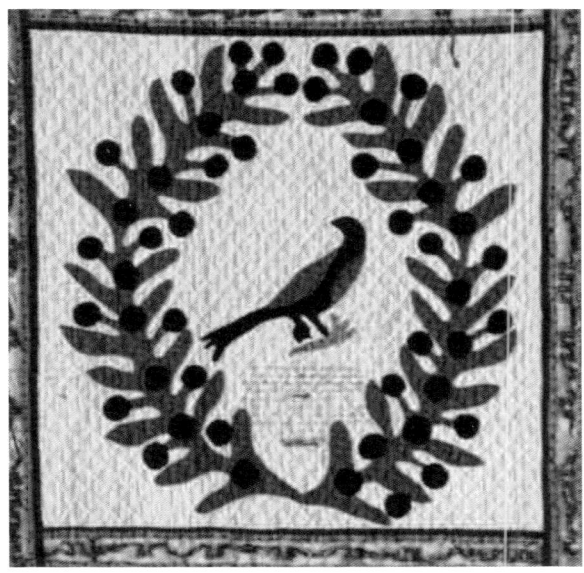

Sampler Album Quilts

A number of terms have been applied to the quilts Barbara Brackman calls sampler album quilts. These terms include presentation quilt, autograph quilt, bride's album quilt, and friendship quilt.[10] Whatever one calls them, these quilts are composed of colorful mixtures of appliquéd and pieced blocks of different patterns, usually sewn and contributed by several different individuals using techniques and fabrics of their choice. Nineteenth-century album quilts were often made to honor an individual, such as a civic leader, a new bride, or a respected clergyman. They were also made to commemorate membership in fraternal organizations or as gifts to people who were leaving a community as a reminder of friends and relatives left behind.

The sampler album quilts classified as "signature quilts" are those that are signed by one or more people. The writing on the quilt may include verses and other annotations that indicate the name of the recipient and the occasion for which the quilt was made. The epitome of the sampler album style is the distinctive Baltimore Album Quilt, a specialty of mainly Methodist quiltmakers, which first appeared in a relatively small area of Maryland in the mid-1840s.[11]

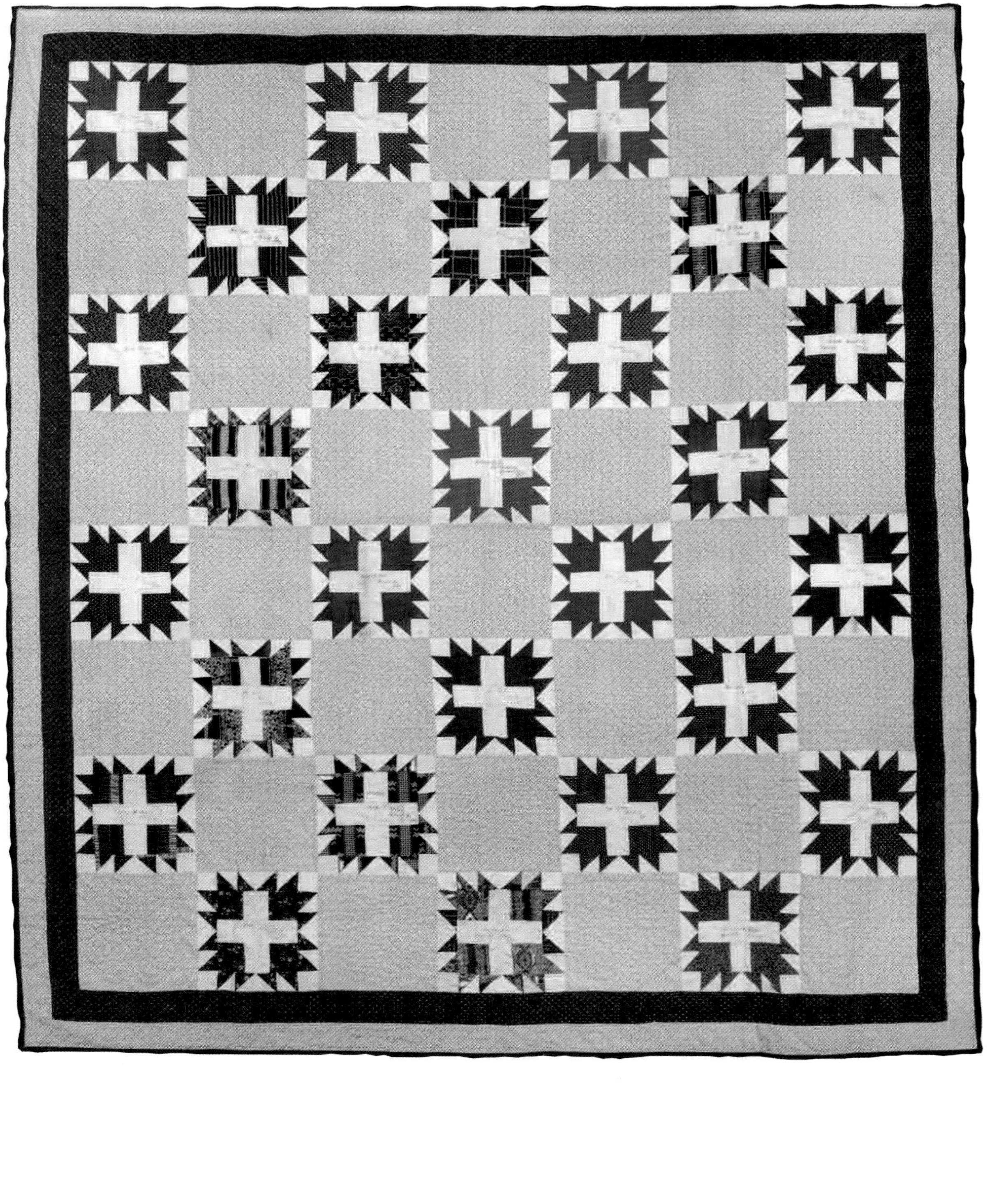

Single-Pattern Friendship Quilts

The friendship quilt, on the other hand, is made of single-pattern blocks, whether pieced, appliquéd, or both. These quilts can be the product of a group effort or that of a single maker who may or may not have solicited blocks from others to add to her quilt. The blocks may be inscribed by a single hand, or each block may display the personal signature of a family member or friend, applied either when the block was made or after the quilt was assembled.[12]

Jane Bentley Kolter has described these quilts as "a friendship offering, and a record of time and memories shared—more homely, in both senses of the word, than the brilliant album quilt."[13] Friendship quilts document networks of relationships, frozen in time, that can include the dead as well as the living, friends as well as family members.

ILLUSTRATION 6. Single-pattern friendship quilt, 1869. Maker unknown, Belmont County, Ohio. 79½" × 89". This quilt is made of modified Bear Paw blocks, some displaying the phrase "Remember Me" dated 1869. Phrases such as "Remember Me" suggest that the quilt was made for someone departing the community due to marriage or for other reasons. This example of a single-pattern friendship quilt has a modern binding and an unusual quilting pattern. It may have been assembled long after the top was completed. The names appearing on the quilt top include Harrison, Glassy, Foreman, Trott, Censhaw, Reinker, Davis, Brandenburg, Bailey, Caton, Jones, McMillan, Cooper, and Glasgow. The names of both men and women appear on the quilt, all on separate blocks. The place names inscribed on the blocks are Pleasant Dell, Ohio; Pine Grove, Ohio; Belmont Co., Ohio; Fulton Co., Illinois: Flushing, Ohio; Perry Co., Ohio; and Bell Air, Ohio. The date April 6, 1859, appears on two blocks. No Quaker connections have been found. Cotton. Pieced, ink inscriptions. Author's collection.

Quaker Signature Quilts

Women belonging to the Religious Society of Friends, like their non-Quaker friends and neighbors, readily adopted quilt styles and patterns that gained popularity in their regional communities.[14] When they moved west into Ohio and other states, they brought with them the quilting traditions they had established elsewhere.

A large number of the nineteenth-century Quakers who moved to Ohio came from the Mid-Atlantic states, where signature quilts had gained widespread popularity during the 1840s. Those who migrated to Ohio during this period brought with them quilting traditions that included both sampler album quilts and single-pattern friendship quilts. Those who had come to Ohio prior to the 1840s learned about these styles through letters, the publications of the day, quilts brought to Ohio by newly arrived settlers, and infrequent but cherished visits to and from relatives and friends back home. Once introduced, both styles gained popularity among Quaker and non-Quaker quiltmakers.

Studies of Quaker-made quilts in New Jersey and the Delaware Valley have provided some evidence that Quaker quiltmakers preferred the single-pattern friendship style to that of the sampler album quilt.[15] Single-pattern friendship quilts seem to have had characteristics that were especially appealing to the Religious Society of Friends, a group devoted to the documentation of life's events. Quakers were prodigious record keepers, as attested by their detailed Monthly, Quarterly, and Yearly Meeting records, and friendship quilts served both to acknowledge major life occurrences and to record networks of relationships within their communities.

The single-pattern style may also have been appealing because it reflected a fundamental Quaker belief that all people were equal, and that no gender, race, or societal position should be elevated above any other. The single-pattern style treated equally all who were represented on the quilt. No one block called special attention to itself, and the sameness of all blocks ensured a sense of unity and equality among those whose names appeared on the quilt.[16]

Quiltmakers produced a large number of single-pattern friendship quilts during the period of their popularity. These quilts were often symbols of friendship, significant life experiences, and shared memories. Among Quaker quiltmakers, these quilts also provided the means to record family and community ties when life's circumstances caused disruption within their community, when they felt a need to affirm religious or social commitments, when marriage occurred within the religious group, or when members of their community moved away.

A doctrinal schism occurred within the Religious Society of Friends in 1827, causing a major disruption that affected the lives of individual Quakers and their communities and profoundly tested their religious commitments. The schism divided the society into two opposing factions: the Orthodox, who wanted to place more authority for spiritual guidance and decision making in the hands of church elders and the scriptures; and the Hicksites, who maintained that primary spiritual guidance must come from the "Inner Light" invested by God in all people.[17] This doctrinal separation not only affected the religious community as a whole, it also divided individual families in which some members chose to remain Orthodox while others elected to become Hicksites. Those choosing to follow the teachings of Elias Hicks were disowned by the Orthodox faction and, in some cases, were ousted from their Monthly Meeting houses. These ejected members found themselves having to rebuild their religious communities without friends and family members who remained Orthodox.

A similar situation shook the Quaker community again in 1854, when the followers of Joseph John Gurney, a British Quaker philanthropist who favored the evangelical approach to spiritual realization, separated from the conservative Friends led by the American John Wilbur. The resulting factions were called Gurneyites and Wilburites, the latter more closely aligned to the teachings of the prior Hicksites. Some years after this schism, a young woman in Ohio, Elizabeth Stanton, made a single-pattern friendship quilt (illustration 7) bearing the names of her Wilburite family and friends to affirm their ties to this religious faction and its doctrine.[18]

ILLUSTRATION 7. Ohio Star quilt, 1859–65. Barnesville, Belmont County, Ohio. 86" × 83". This single-pattern friendship quilt was made by Elizabeth Stanton and affirmed her family ties to the Wilburite faction of the Religious Society of Friends. The names of husbands and wives who appear on this quilt are placed together on single blocks, a characteristic of Quaker signature quilts. Cotton. Pieced, ink inscriptions. Collection of the Ohio Historical Society, Columbus, Ohio.

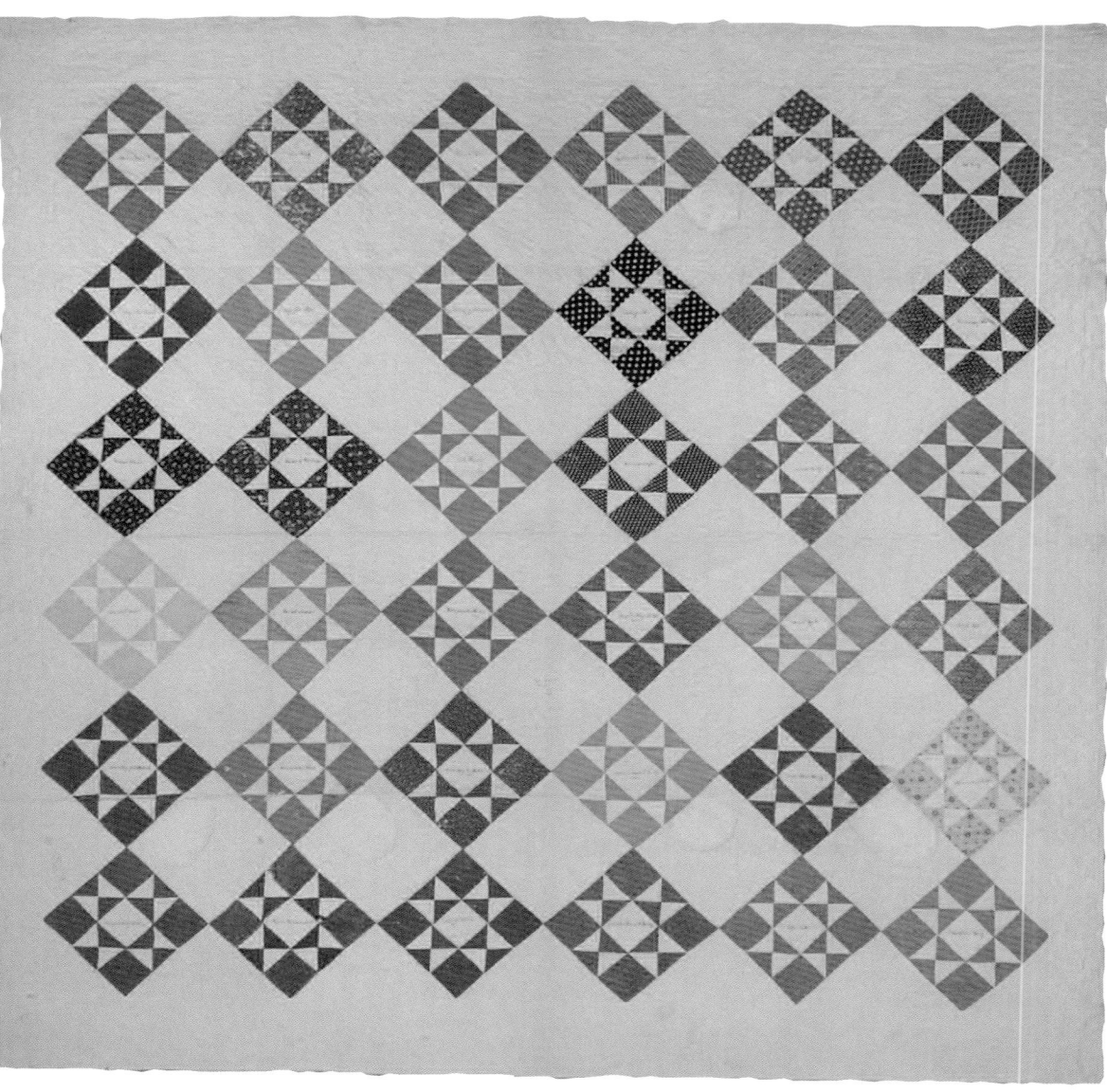

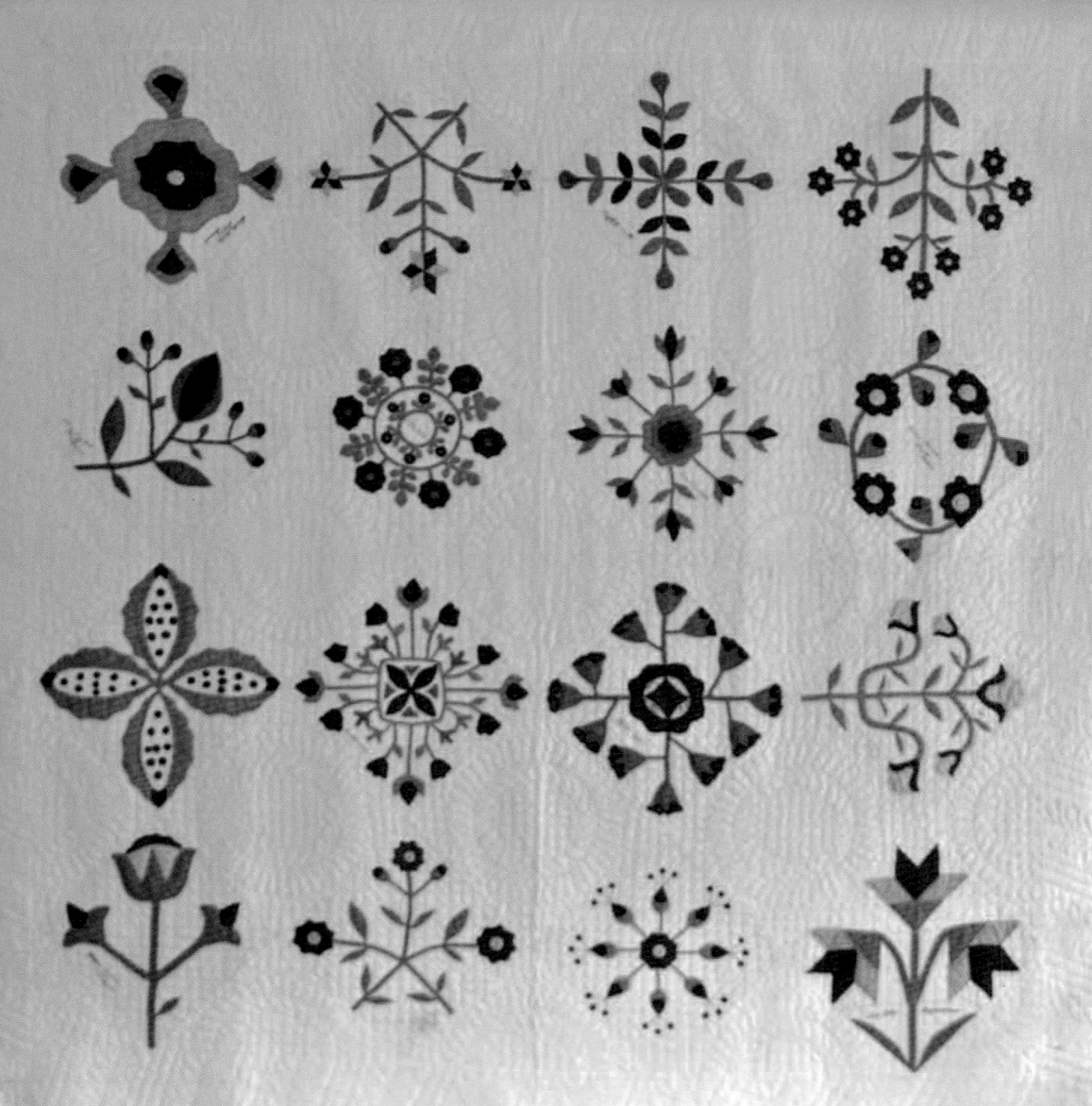

The use of a signature quilt to document both religious and social commitment is described by Ricky Clark in her article "Making a Case for the Abolitionist Quilt," published in the July/August 1995 issue of *Piecework*. The quilt she discusses was made by Quaker women from Clinton County, Ohio, and Wayne County, Indiana, who had been disowned from their Monthly Meetings for their outspoken support of the antislavery cause. Once ousted, they joined the Newport Monthly Meeting of Anti-Slavery Friends just over the Ohio border in Indiana. Their signed sampler album quilt is, in effect, a statement of their antislavery sentiment and, as stated in the article, may have been made to strengthen the bonds of those named on it during a difficult time.

On other occasions, Quaker signature quilts were made in honor of the impending marriage of a young woman in their religious community. Traditionally, the quilt was made by the young woman's female friends and family members, each contributing a signed quilt block to be added to the whole. When completed, the quilt acknowledged not only the serious and life-changing event the woman was about to experience, but also the bonds of love, friendship, and religious community that existed among the women who contributed to the quilt. If the bride was to remain in her loving community as a wife, the quilt served to strengthen her ties to this community. If she was to move away as a result of her marriage, the quilt provided a trea-

sured reminder of a still-loving community of "sisters" that she could take with her as she began a new life elsewhere.

One example of such a quilt was that made in 1847 for Ann Coppock, the daughter of Jehu and Judith Stanley Coppock of Knox Township, Columbiana County, Ohio. Ann was born on November 9, 1828, and married John Butler of Marlboro, Stark County, on May 27, 1847, in Upper Springfield Monthly Meeting. She was eighteen years old at the time of her marriage.[19]

Ann's quilt, a holding of the Ohio Historical Society in Columbus, is made up of seventy-two Album Patch blocks inscribed with eighty-six names. The dates 1846 and 1847 are also inscribed on some of the blocks, and at the very top in the two center edging triangles are the words "Ann Coppock 1847" and "Ann Coppock's quilt."

The names of thirty-two men and fifty-four women appear on Ann's quilt. The men were Ann's in-laws, young men soon to be married to some of the women named on the quilt, male cousins, Ann's fiancée John Butler, and, in one case, the father of a friend. Almost all of the women named on Ann's quilt were from her mother's side of the family.[20] The ages, in early 1847, of forty-six of the women could be determined. Below is the distribution of these women, by age.

Between 6 and 15 years of age	9
Between 16 and 29 years of age	26 (57%)
Between 30 and 40 years of age	7
Over 40 years of age	4

Two of the women in the last age group were Ann's grandmother, Unity Crew Stanley, who was eighty-six when her quilt block was inscribed in 1846, and Ann's mother, Judith Stanley Coppock,

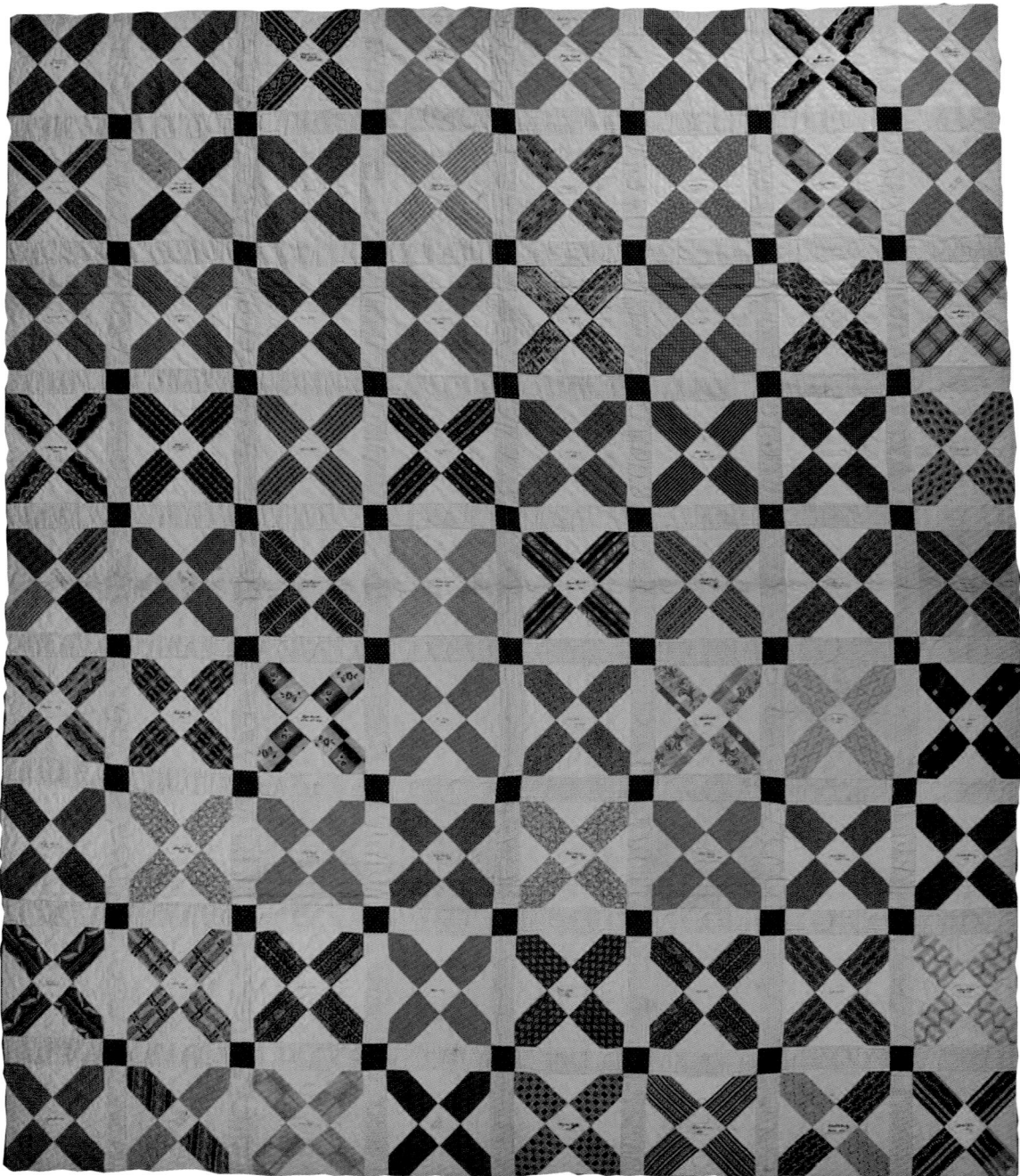

who was fifty-four. Of the twenty-six young women between the ages of sixteen and twenty-nine, all but five were unmarried at the time the quilt was made. This collection of predominantly young women from her mother's side of the family, along with Ann's maternal grandmother and mother, suggest a group of close relatives and friends whom Ann could continue to rely on for support after her marriage.[21]

The number of Quaker signature quilts made to affirm support at the time of marriage was probably equaled by those made on the occasion of the departure of a beloved person or family from their long-standing community. The migration of Quaker families to newly opened territories began as early as the late sixteenth century, when they began inhabiting new lands in the Northwest Territory—a territory opened to settlement and proclaimed forever free from slavery by the Ordinance of 1787. The absence of slavery in this new land was one of the many incentives that drew Quaker families, who abhorred the practice of slavery, to migrate north and west. The five territorial states later admitted to the Union, and to which these Quakers moved, were Ohio, Indiana, Illinois, Michigan, and Wisconsin.[22] Hicksite families were among those who migrated to these states in large numbers. They sought, in addition to the absence of slavery, inexpensive and fertile farming lands in areas that were just opening to settlers. By the 1840s, many of the families who had moved into Ohio and the other states of the Northwest Territory were again headed west, seeking fertile and inexpensive land to farm and leaving behind the communities they had formed in earlier times.

Quakers, especially the women, had a profound sense of their community that was based on their worship together and the network of communal support that bound them. Separation from their community of Friends, and friends, represented for them a major life transition. Whether caused by relocating to new territories, marriage, or the need to move on for other reasons, Quaker women in the 1840s, 1850s, and beyond often commemorated departures by documenting, on the face of a quilt, treasured family members and friends who were being left behind.

Ricky Clark, in describing the major functions of friendship quilts, includes the phrase "to counteract the disruption of community."[23] Evidence collected in researching Philena's quilt, and presented throughout this book, indicates that the quilt was made for her after she and her husband decided to leave Columbiana County and move farther west. The quilt she took with her when they left their community in Ohio symbolically preserved the relationships recorded on it for the rest of Philena's life.

ILLUSTRATION 9. *Ann Coppock's Quilt*, 1847. This single-pattern friendship quilt was made for Ann Coppock to commemorate her marriage to John Butler, in Knox Township, Columbiana County, Ohio. 92 ½" × 103". Ann's quilt is made up of seventy-two Album Patch blocks made from a variety of prints. Cotton. Pieced, ink inscriptions. Collection of the Ohio Historical Society, Columbus, Ohio.

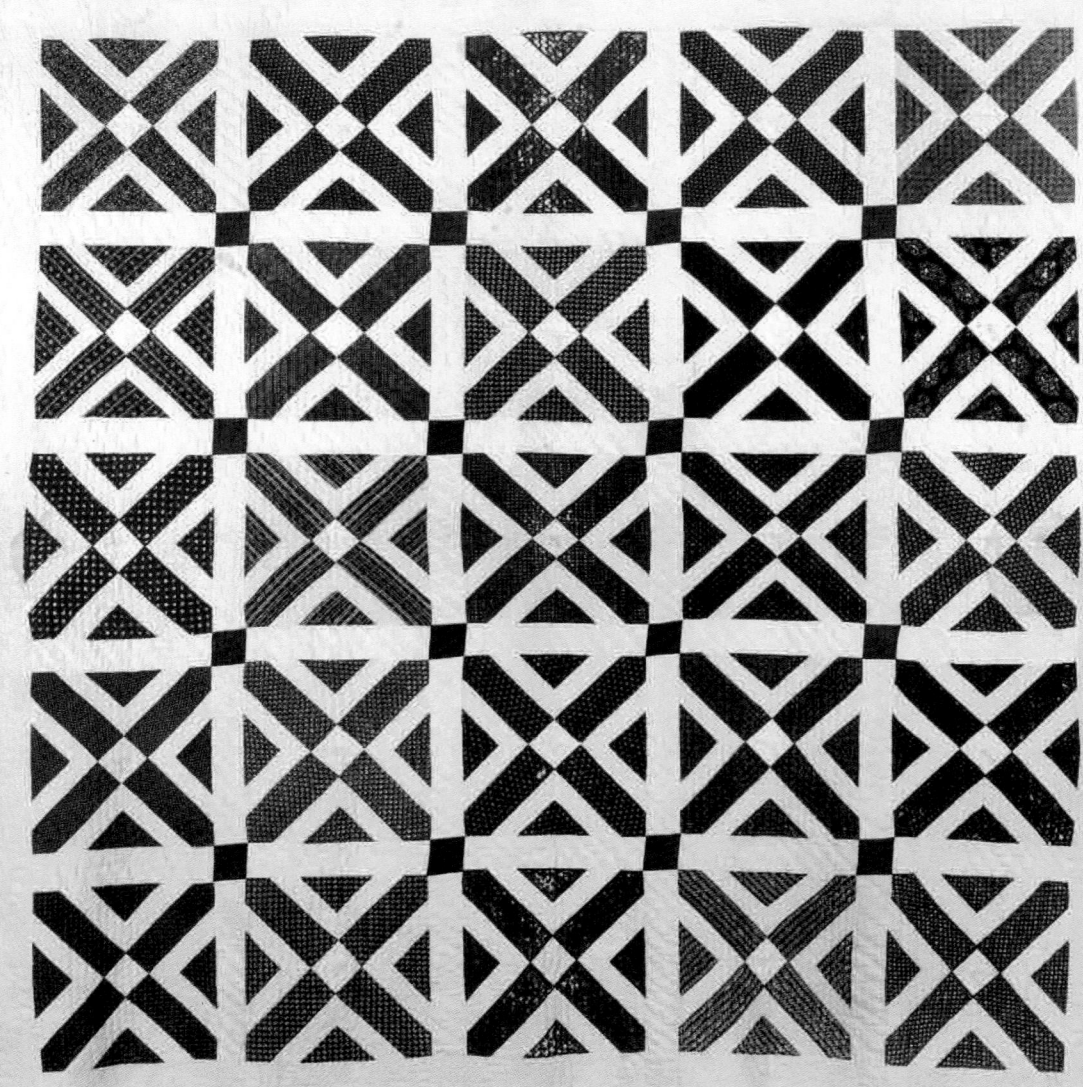

Philena's Quilt

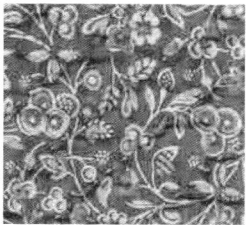

The Fabrics

ALL OF THE FABRICS IN PHILENA'S QUILT ARE cotton. They include a white used in the pieced blocks, for the sashes, and for the quilt backing. The sash connecting squares and the binding are two different greens with overdyed black decorative elements. (See fabrics nos. 22 and 23 in illustration 13 at the end of this section.) The binding fabric is fading to blue. The connecting-square fabric is fading to yellow. The black in the connecting-square fabric appears as a smudgy brown-black. Both fabrics are consistent with overdyed greens of the 1830s–60s.[1]

ILLUSTRATION 10. *Philena's Friendship Quilt*, 1853. Single-pattern friendship quilt made for Philena Cooper Hambleton, Butler Township, Columbiana County, Ohio. 83½" × 83½". The quilt's twenty-five blocks are a variation of the Album Patch. The quilt is hand-pieced and hand-quilted with six to nine stitches per inch. The body of the quilt is closely quilted, and the border is quilted using a running-feather border design. Instructions for making a replica of Philena's quilt are provided at the end of the book. Cotton. Pieced, ink inscriptions. Author's collection.

The remaining fabrics are twenty different prints and one solid fabric that appear, stylistically, to be "Turkey reds."[2] The Turkey-red prints that were referred to as "calicoes" displayed small-scale printed designs featuring mainly black, blue, green, and yellow elements.[3] Brilliant reds such as these were used extensively in the mid-nineteenth century both in the distinctive green-and-red appliquéd quilts of the period and in friendship quilts.

The red fabrics featured in Philena's quilt are shown in illustration 13 as numbers 1 through 21. Only three of the fabrics (nos. 1, 2, and 3) were used in more than one block. Some of the fabrics are in poor condition and display the sort of damage Barbara Brackman describes as resulting from fabric "tendering" caused by discharge-process dyes and chemicals.[4] This process disintegrates the fabric where overdyeing occurred. On Philena's quilt, this damage appears mainly where there are overdyed blacks.

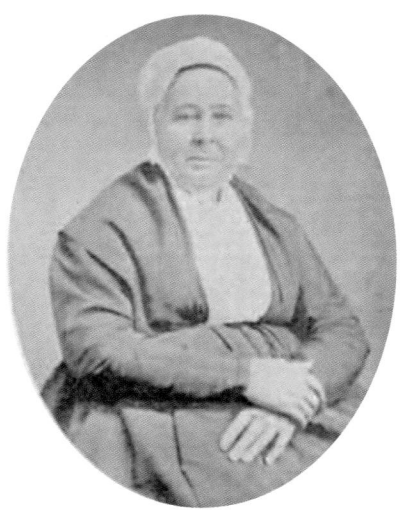

ILLUSTRATION II. Philena's mother-in-law, Ann Hanna Hambleton (July 30, 1797–March 10, 1867), wearing dress typical of the Hicksite women living in rural Ohio during the mid-nineteenth century. Ann was probably in her fifties when the photograph was taken. Photograph from Charles E. Rice, *A History of the Hanna Family* (Damascus, OH: Aden Pim and Son, Printers, 1905), 108.

Choice of Fabric

The choice of brilliant red fabrics for a Quaker quilt may seem incongruous with the teachings of the Religious Society of Friends. Codes of behavior for Friends were defined and issued by the Yearly Meetings established as the highest organizational level within the faith. Yearly Meetings had jurisdiction over Quarterly, Monthly, and Preparative Meetings taking place within particular geographical areas. Regional codes of behavior in both England and America were printed as "general advices" in publications called "disciplines" that were issued by the Yearly Meetings.

The Ohio Yearly Meeting, held at Mount Pleasant in 1819, issued the following advice concerning worldly goods: "To observe due moderation in the furniture of their housing and to avoid superfluity in their manner of living."[5] The avoidance of superfluity applied to dress as well as to other aspects of Quaker life, and superfluity in dress was regionally defined by the general advices of the re-

lated Yearly Meetings as well as by personal preference. In some places and times, the use of buttons, ribbons, brightly colored fabrics, long scarves, and "gaudy stomachers" were considered superfluous. In the end most, but not all, American Quakers adopted a style of dress that "combined personal belief and taste, with an understanding of what was allowable within one's own meeting."[6]

Although both men's and women's dress varied regionally and over time, the typical plain dress for Quaker women in the mid-nineteenth century consisted of a simple bonnet and a modest, floor-length dress in subdued tones, often with a cream-colored shawl or bodice-insert.[7] The modesty of this dress, however, did not prevent Quakers from purchasing or making clothing from the best materials they could afford. Quaker women wore dresses and bonnets made of both expensive silks and more durable fabrics of fine quality, but the dictates of moderation prevented them from following the latest styles. The purpose was to avoid attracting attention to oneself through either the fashionable style of one's clothing or fabrics of "showy" color. Those who did

ILLUSTRATION 12. Sawtooth Bar Quaker quilt, 1886. Known as the *Starr Quilt*. This quilt was made by members of the Short Creek Monthly Meeting as a wedding gift to Gilbert McGrew and Eliza Hall, who married April 29, 1886, in Harrisville, Jefferson County, Ohio. 80" × 80". It is an example of a Quaker-made silk quilt in muted tones. The silks are olive green and brown. The quilt is backed with polished, tan cotton. Pieced. Collection of the Ohio Historical Society, Columbus, Ohio.

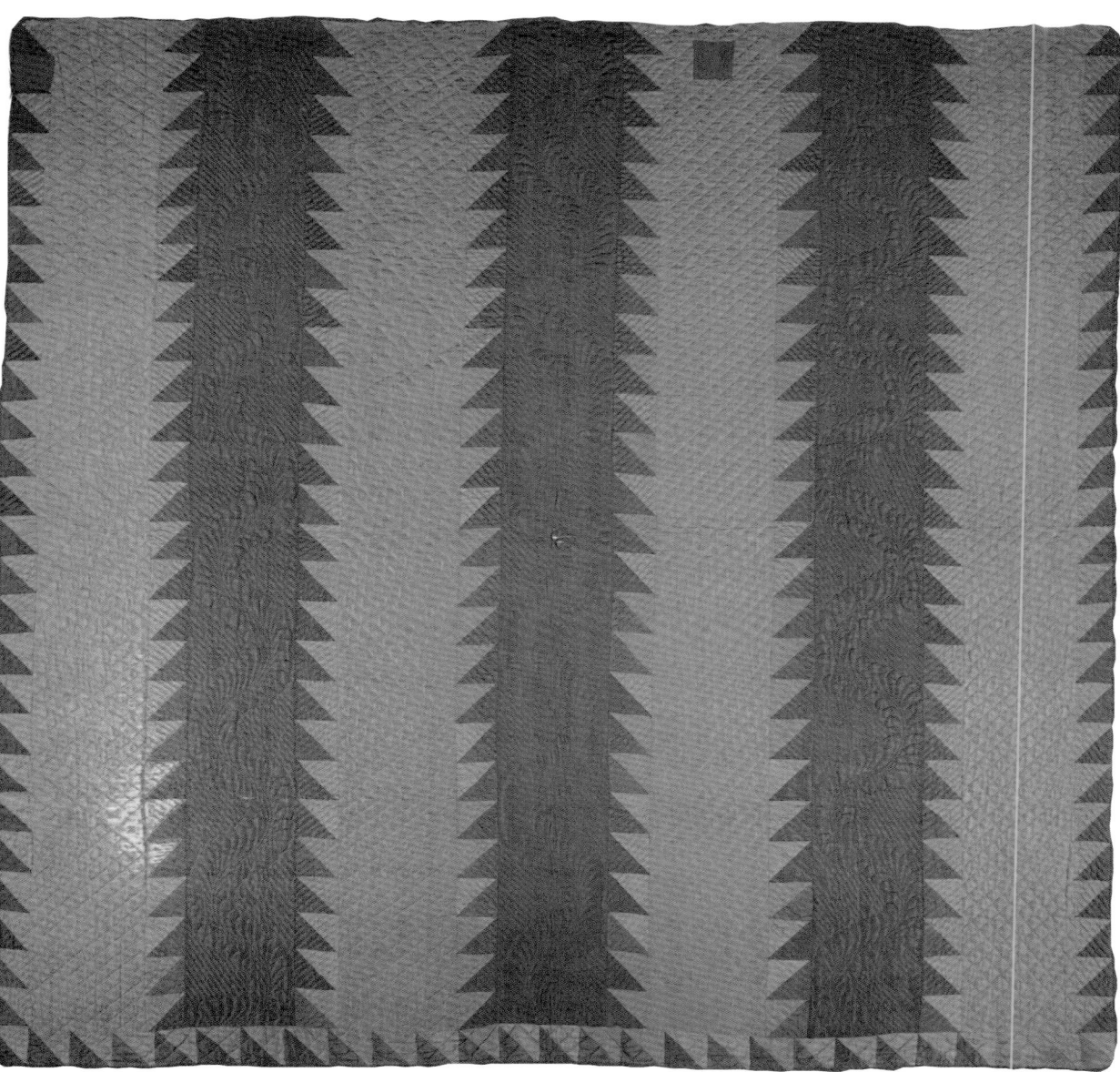

not practice moderation were considered "gay Friends," in contrast to the "plain Friends" who rigorously followed early dictates of dress.[8]

When it came to household goods, and especially quilts, Quakers often chose items or fabrics that displayed vibrant color in seeming contradiction to the plainness advocated by their disciplines and the muted colors of their clothing. This contradiction is discussed at some length by Patricia J. Keller in contrasting the early Quaker quilts of the Delaware Valley made with expensive silks of muted colors with those of the 1840s made from readily available, inexpensive bright cotton prints.[9] It is also addressed by Jessica F. Nicoll, who notes that historians have long commented on the discrepancy between the advocated plainness for Friends and the actual material objects they made or accumulated for everyday use.[10] The fact remains that, for whatever religious, personal, social, or community reason, extant examples of Quaker quilts display the general use of fine quality, and sometimes brightly colored, fabrics for their sampler album and single-pattern friendship quilts.

The selection of red fabrics for Philena's quilt is not unusual for either Quaker or non-Quaker friendship quilts. There appears to have been a preference for the use of reds, in general, for both friendship and sampler album quilts during the mid-nineteenth century. This is attested to by the number of quilts containing red fabric that are shown in quilt publications.[11]

ILLUSTRATION 13. Fabrics in Philena's quilt (pages 22–25)

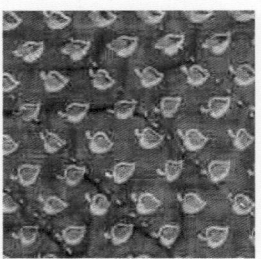

FABRIC NO. 1

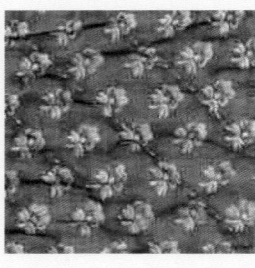

FABRIC NO. 4

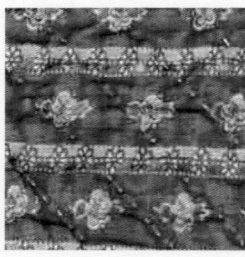

FABRIC NO. 7

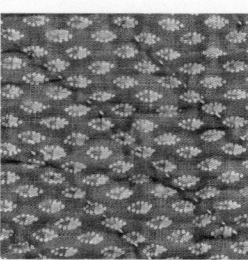

FABRIC NO. 10

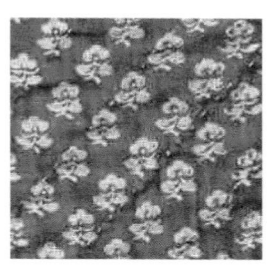

FABRIC NO. 2

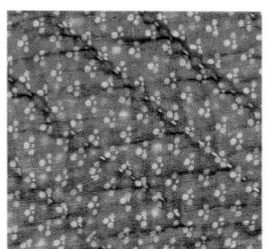

FABRIC NO. 3

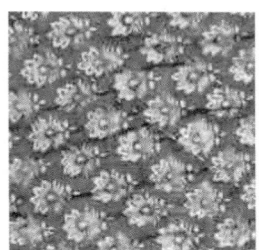

FABRIC NO. 5

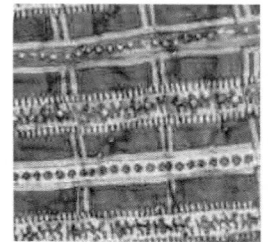

FABRIC NO. 6

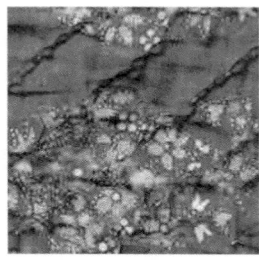

FABRIC NO. 8

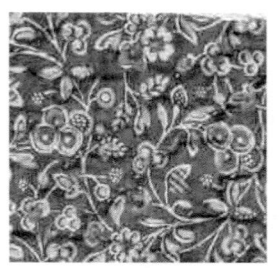

FABRIC NO. 9

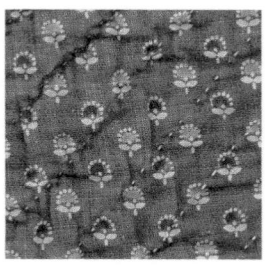

FABRIC NO. 11

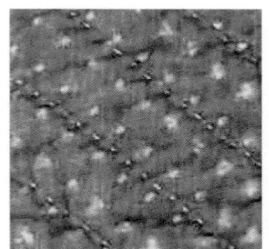

FABRIC NO. 12

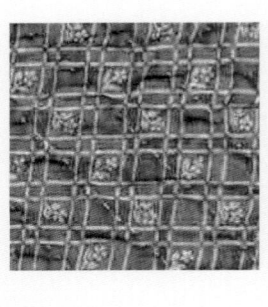

FABRIC NO. 13

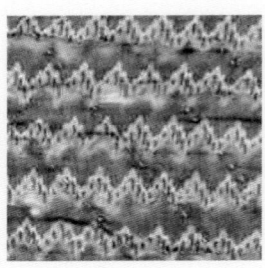

FABRIC NO. 14

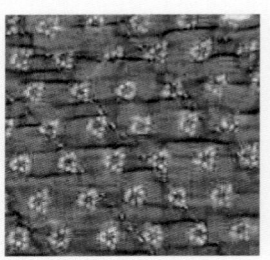

FABRIC NO. 15

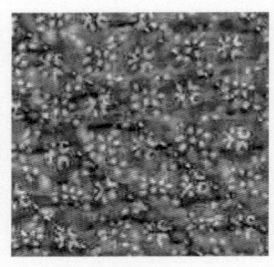

FABRIC NO. 16

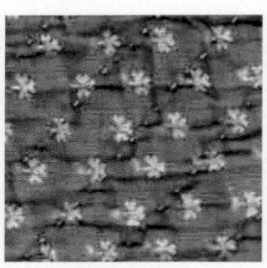

FABRIC NO. 17

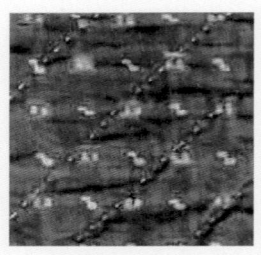

FABRIC NO. 18

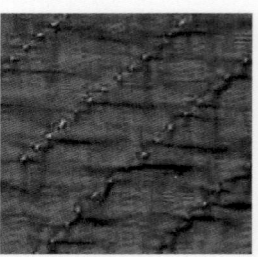

FABRIC NO. 19

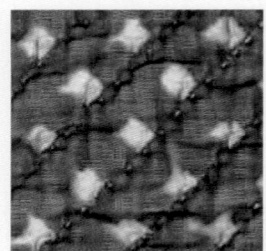

FABRIC NO. 20

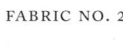

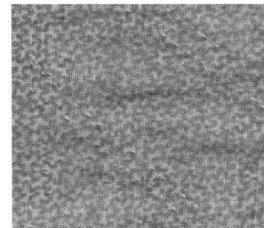

FABRIC NO. 21

FABRIC NO. 22

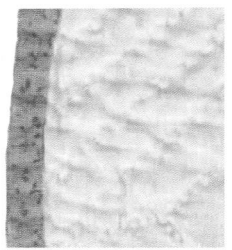

FABRIC NO. 23

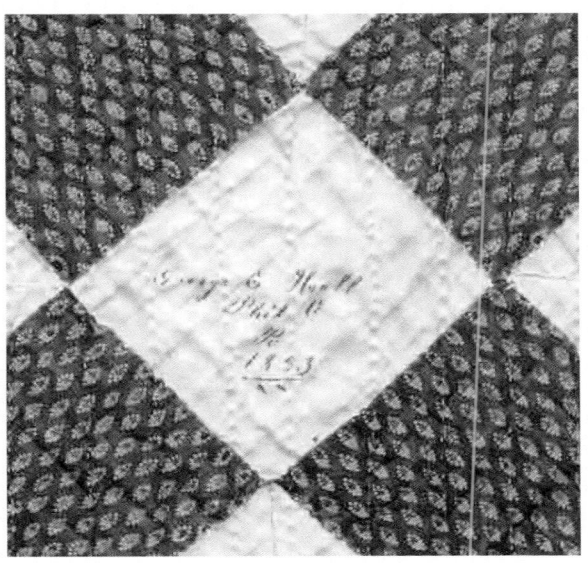

Above: Quilting that appears in the border and on the sashes.

Right: The most legible writing on the quilt.

Philena's Community of Family and Friends

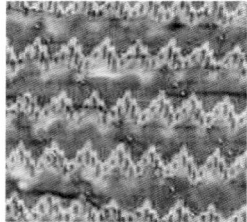

THE TWENTY-FIVE BLOCKS IN PHILENA'S QUILT are arranged in a five-by-five grid. All blocks display the names of one or more persons. One block is water-damaged, and the names cannot be read. One of the twenty-five blocks records the death of Philena's father. Twenty-one of the blocks list the date 1853, and twenty-one include a town, county, and state for those named. These last designations appear to be where those named on the quilt were at the time the quilt was inscribed. For most, the locations were where the people actually lived in the early 1850s, as confirmed by 1850 census records. For five of them, however, the inscriptions list locations that were either temporary or unknown.

Mary and Jesse Hambleton, who occupy the center block of the quilt, are listed as being in New Garden, Columbiana County, Ohio, at the time their block was inscribed, but their permanent residence was in Cecil County, Maryland.[1] (The possible significance of placing the names of Mary and Jesse on the center block of the quilt is discussed later.) Three others, all men, are listed as being

Anywhere, Everywhere, and a Good Many Places, even though they all resided in Columbiana County, Ohio, at the time of the 1850 census. Two of them, John Hoyt and Whitson Milton Cooper, were Philena's brothers. The third, Thomas Clarkson Hambleton, was a brother of her husband, Osborn. The actual whereabouts of these close relatives seems to have been unknown at the time the quilt was inscribed. (See illustration 14 for the names and other information written on the quilt in black ink.[2])

An Extended Community

The names inscribed on Philena's quilt represent an extensive family and community network based, at the time, in Butler and West townships. Butler Township, where Philena lived after her marriage, was founded in 1806 as one of the eighteen townships that now make up Columbiana County. This rural township contained 1,711 inhabitants in 1840 and only 1,560 in 1880. The small town of Winona

Joseph & Phebe Windell New Garden Columbiana Ohio 1853	Calvin A. Cooper Orangeburgh Mason Co. KY	M.A. & M.L. Clempson Lynchburgh Columbiana Ohio 1853	Wm. & Martha Cooper Fairfield Columbiana Ohio 1853	Thomas & Phebe Hall Cedar Co. Io 1853
Peter & Margaret Ward New Garden Col. Co. Ohio 1853	Joel G. & Phebe A. Hambleton Harrisville Harrison Co. Ohio 1853	Reuben & Rachel Clempson Lynchburgh Col. Co. Ohio 1853	Levi & Mary H. Hambleton Marlboro Stark Co. Ohio 1853	Stephen & Mary Mendenhall Marlboro Stark Co. Ohio 1853
Names Obliterated New Garden Columbiana Ohio	Cath. H. Hambleton New Garden Columbiana Ohio 1853	Mary & Jesse Hambleton New Garden Columbiana Ohio 1853	Rachel Hambleton New Garden Col. Co. Ohio 1853	Sarah A. Griffith New Garden Columbiana Ohio 1853
George E. Hall Phil. Co. Pa 1853	Martha K. Hambleton New Garden Col. Co. Ohio 1853	Whitson Cooper Died in the Year 1835	Thomas C. Hambleton Anywhere No. Co. 1853	John Ward Marlboro Stark Co. Ohio 1853
Alfred & Sarah Hall Cedar Co. Io	Whitson M. Cooper Good Many Places Ohio 1853	C.H. & A.A. Clempson Lynchburgh Col. Co. Ohio 1853	John H. Cooper Everywhere No. Co. 1853	Benj. & Lydia Windle Franklin Square Col. Co. Ohio 1853

ILLUSTRATION 14. Names and other information written on Philena's quilt

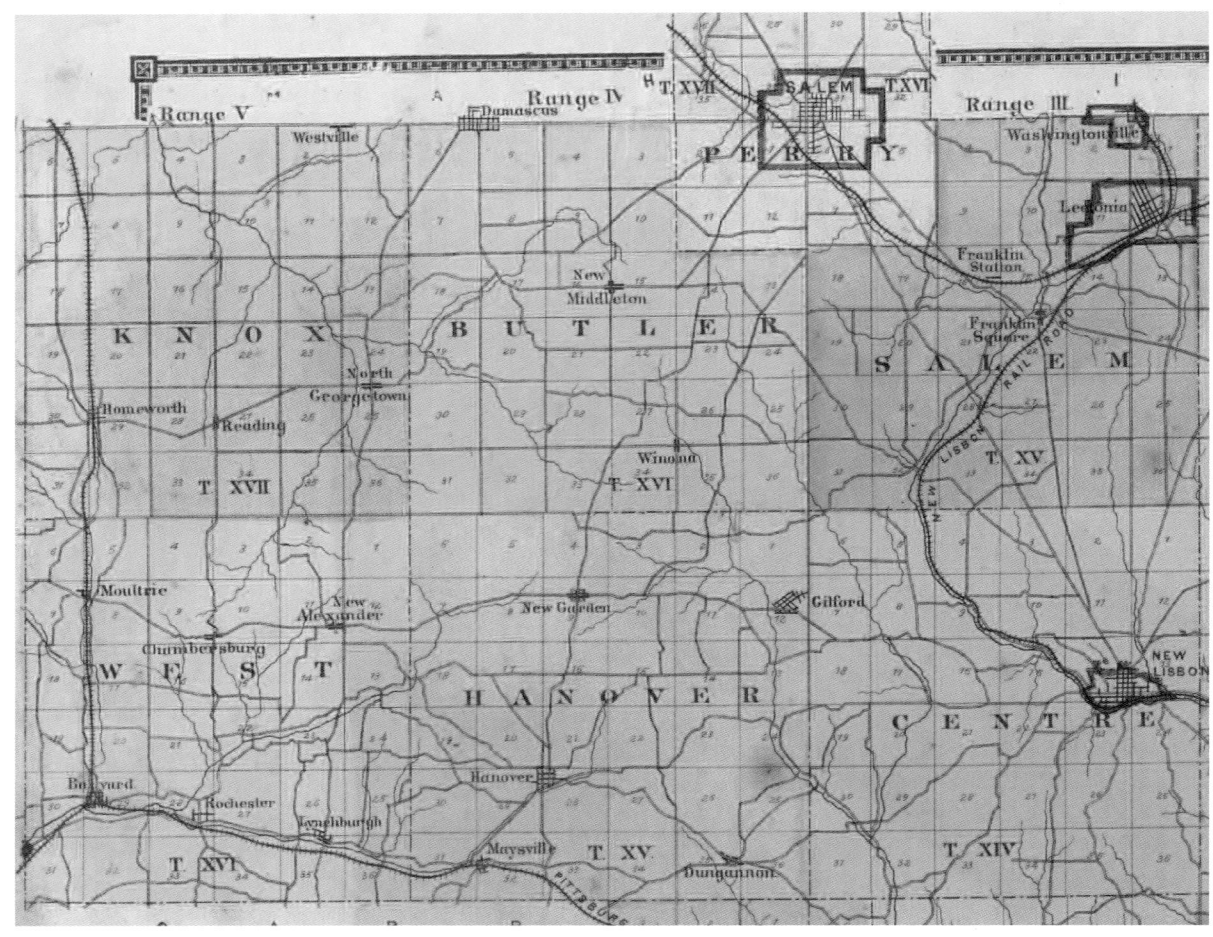

ILLUSTRATION 15. Map of northwestern Columbiana County townships from *Walling's Atlas of Ohio, Counties of Columbiana, Jefferson, Carroll and Harrison,* 1870. Note the locations and proximity of Salem (Perry Township), New Garden (Hanover Township), New Lisbon (Centre Township), and Lynchburg (West Township). All of the townships shown except Perry, Butler, and Salem are six miles square. Butler and Salem townships lost a small portion of their land when Perry Township was created in 1832. Knox Township, where Ann Coppock's quilt was made, borders on Butler Township to the west.

was situated two miles from the Hambleton home, but in 1853, when the quilt was completed, the nearest post office was located at New Garden, about three and a half miles to the southeast in Hanover Township. Philena's mother, with her second husband, Reuben Clempson, two of Philena's brothers, and her half-sisters, lived in the small town of Lynchburg in West Township southwest of Butler Township. West Township, too, was mainly farm country. The largest towns in the area were Salem, to the north of Butler Township in Perry Township, and New Lisbon, to the southeast in Centre Township. In 1840, the population of Columbiana County was 40,394, but this figure declined when five of Columbiana County's original townships were incorporated into Mahoning County in 1846.[3]

All of the people named on Philena's quilt had either familial or community ties to the Hambleton or Cooper families. Most of the people, but not all, were members of the Religious Society of Friends. The names placed on individual blocks include husbands and wives together, single individuals of both sexes, and, curiously in one case, a female relative whose husband was still alive but who is listed on a single block with one of her sons.

Two of those named had died before the quilt was completed in 1853. One of them, Peter Ward, was listed on the quilt along with his second wife, Margaret. The other, Whitson Cooper, was Philena's father, the father of five other people named on the quilt, the brother of two of the women listed, and the former husband of a third. While it may seem odd today to include deceased family members on friendship quilts, it was a common practice among quiltmakers of the nineteenth century. The passing of those who went before did not diminish the importance of their role in a family's history, their past relationship with living family members, or the desire that they be remembered.

In addition to relatives, the people named on Philena's quilt included friends and neighbors. Some of them owned land with shared boundaries, and all seemed to hold common religious and political sentiments.[4] Members of several of these families came to Ohio from Chester County, Pennsylvania, and some were active, along with Philena, her husband Osborn, and two other members of the Hambleton family, in both the Ohio Anti-Slavery Society and the New Garden Anti-Slavery Society founded in Hanover Township in 1824.[5] (See illustration 17 for a profile of the community represented on Philena's quilt.)

Both Philena's quilt and Ann Coppock's exhibit key characteristics of Quaker friendship quilts. These characteristics include name inscriptions of numbers of people who have a variety of relationships and who live in more than one location. Delaware Valley quilts studied by Jessica F. Nicoll prompted this observation: "Quaker-made quilts record much larger groups of people than other quilts and present a more complete community picture by including the names of men, women and children."[6] Another characteristic of Quaker quilts was to record the names of husband and wife together on a single block—a practice not usually observed outside of the Religious Society of Friends.[7]

In contrast to Ann Coppock's quilt, which names eighty-six, only thirty-nine people are named on Philena's quilt. Females and males are essentially equal in representation, with twenty women and nineteen men. Twelve of each sex are husband and wife, accounting for twenty-four of the thirty-nine

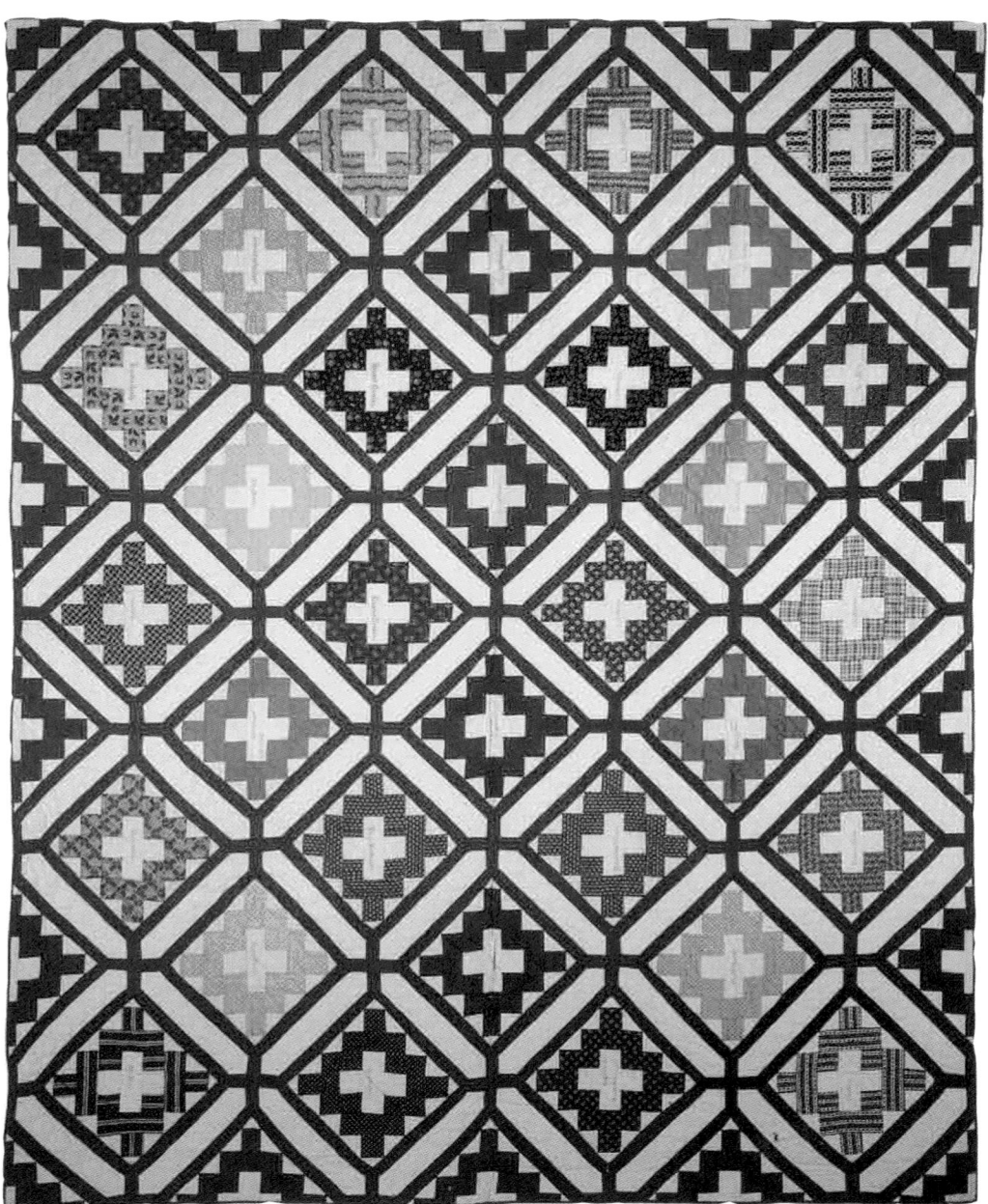

people named—62 percent, compared to twenty-six out of eighty-six (30 percent) married people on Ann Coppock's quilt. Below is the age distribution of the women on Philena's quilt (ages as of early 1853).

Between 9 and 15 years of age	3
Between 16 and 29 years of age	6
Between 30 and 40 years of age	4
Over 40 years of age	7

As with the distribution of men and women on the two quilts, the women on Philena's quilt were more evenly distributed among age groups (see chapter 2 for the Coppock quilt illustrations).

The differences in the communities represented on Ann Coppock's quilt and that of Philena are not surprising. Ann was eighteen years old when her quilt was made, and the names on her quilt represent the family and friends of a young girl about to be married within her existing rural community. Predominant are close female family members, cousins, and friends of both sexes who were unmarried and within Ann's age range. Ann had yet to participate in her community as a married adult and the mother of children. The community her quilt represents was inner-directed and focused primarily on the female members of her family. No

ILLUSTRATION 16. *Margaret Weeden Quilt,* 1894. This quilt was made by Margaret Weeden for her daughter, Cora, a year after Cora's marriage to Charles Mills, Columbus, Ohio, 101½" × 81½". The names on the quilt include those of six ancestors. Including the names of deceased family members was a common practice in the nineteenth century. Cotton. Pieced, ink inscriptions. Collection of the Lorain County Historical Society, Elyria, Ohio; photo courtesy of the Herbert F. Johnson Museum of Art, Cornell University.

deceased individuals were named on her quilt—not even her father, who had died just five years earlier. The community represented on Ann's marriage quilt symbolizes the carefree days of youth and the continuation of a promising future among family and friends in the area in which she grew up.

Philena was thirty years old when her quilt was completed. She was a wife and the mother of two children. She would soon be leaving a community in which she had developed mature relationships that extended beyond her immediate family. She was leaving behind a mother, her only sister, four young half-sisters, and friends who shared her abolitionist sentiments and had experienced, with her and her husband, the dangers of antislavery activism. The community on Philena's quilt symbolizes the past, the friends and relatives she was leaving behind, and the memory of a father who had died unexpectedly almost twenty years before.

The people named on Ann's quilt and Philena's quilt reflect the circumstances under which each quilt was made and represent distinct differences in the ages and life experiences of each of these women.

Name Placement

The names placed on friendship quilts may be recorded on individual blocks prior to their being joined together, or may be recorded on the quilt top after the blocks are joined. The location of names on a quilt top, relative to one another, may be the result of design considerations, may simply be random, or may impart information about the closeness or types of relationships of the people named. In the last case, familial relationships may be indicated by the proximity or groupings of names.

Names	Relationship		Religion		Family From		Present/Past Neighbor		Abolitionist		
	Blood	In-Law	Quaker	Other	Chester Co, PA	Bradford MM	w/in 2 miles	w/in 5-20	NGASS	UGRR	Other
Clempson											
Reuben	X				X	X		X			
Rachel Cooper		X	H	X	X	X		X			
Mary A.	X				X	X		X			
Maria Louisa	X				X	X		X			
Cecilia	X				X	X		X			
Amelia A.	X				X	X		X			
Cooper											
Whitson	X		O		X	X		X			
William	X				X	X		X			
Calvin A.	X				X	X		X			
John H.	X				X	X					
Whitson M.	X				X	X	X				
Griffith											
William Jr.		X	H				X		X		
Mary Votaw			H				X		X		
Sarah A.			H				X				
Hall											
Thomas V.	X		H		X	X		X			
Phebe	X		H		X	X		X			
Alfred			H		X	X		X			
Sarah Farrington		X	H					X			
George E.		X	H		X						

ILLUSTRATION 17. Profile of Philena's Community

Names	Relationship		Religion		Family From		Present/Past Neighbor		Abolitionist		
	Blood	In-Law	Quaker	Other	Chester Co. PA	Bradford MM	w/in 2 miles	w/in 5-20	NGASS	UGRR	Other
Hambleton											
Joel G.	X	X	H		X		X				X
Phebe Cooper	X		H		X	X		X			X
Rachel		X	H		X		X		X		
Levi		X	H		X			X			
Mary H. Hall		X	H		X			X			
Catherine		X		X	X		X				
Martha K.		X		X	X		X				
Thomas C.		X			X		X				
Mary Conard		X	H		X						
Jesse		X	H		X						
Mendenhall											
Stephen G.			H		X			X		X	
Mary Thomas			H		X			X		X	
Ward											
Peter				X	X		X				
Margaret				X	X		X				
John					X		X				
Windle											
Benjamin	X	X	O		X	X		X			
Lydia Cooper	X				X			X			
Joseph J.		X	H		X		X				
Phebe Dutton		X	H		X		X				
Hambletons Not on Quilt											
Philena (recipient)			H		X	X					X
Osborn (husband)			H		X				X	X	X
Benjamin		X	H		X				X	X	
Ann Hanna (Osborn's parents)		X	H		X					X	

Key to Headings:

Relationship = relationship to Philena

Religion = Quaker where H = Hicksite, O = Orthodox and Other Religion

Family From = indicates persons who had family who had lived in Chester Co. PA & attended the Bradford Monthly Meeting before moving to Ohio

Neighbor = indicates people who lived within 2 or 5-20 miles of Philena and Osborn at the time the quilt was made or before

Abolitionist = documented abolitionist; NGASS = member of the New Garden Anti-Slavery Society; UGRR = operator on the Underground Railroad; Other = member/founder of other anti-slavery society

In Baltimore-style album quilts, block placement is often dictated by considerations of color and block construction, without regard to the names appearing on the blocks. The visual impact of block placement can also be a factor when arranging single-pattern blocks that are made up of a variety of colored and figured fabrics. In such cases, the placement of names on a quilt's surface tends to be somewhat random. The random placement of names on a quilt's surface may also occur when the names designate people belonging to a specific group of individuals who have equal status, such as on fund-raising quilts.

If a quilt's blocks are each constructed in the same pattern with the same or similar fabrics, however, the quiltmaker has more opportunity to group or otherwise arrange the names appearing on these blocks without regard to visual impact. Many nineteenth-century signature quilts provide examples of the deliberate grouping of family names to illustrate their importance to the quiltmaker. Included in these are the Quaker quilts made for Ann Coppock (illustration 9), that made by Elizabeth Stanton (illustration 7), and a silk quilt in the collections of the Winterthur Museum and Country Estate in Delaware.

Ann Coppock's quilt displays the names of many of Ann's family members. Those closest to her, however, are placed at the top of the quilt in the first and second horizontal rows. The names of her grandmother and mother are placed in the center of the first row, directly beneath the top edge where Ann's name appears. Ann's sisters and their husbands are in the top two rows, along with some of her female cousins, the daughters of her mother's brothers. The names of more cousins, as well as

more distant relatives and friends, are scattered over the rest of the quilt. Most of the single men named on the quilt appear in the sixth row down, with others scattered over the remaining three rows at the bottom of the quilt.

Elizabeth Stanton abutted the plain block in the center of her quilt, which bears the notation "Lizzie / Stanton / Barnesville / Ohio / 1865," with four blocks that are inscribed with the names of her immediate family members. Elsewhere, she arranged the blocks of other individuals in family groups.[8]

The silk quilt at Winterthur was made in Philadelphia in 1851 to mark the marriage of Sarah Williams to Samuel Emlen. In this case, the quiltmaker positioned the names of close family members in the center, with name groupings of more distant relatives and friends moving to the outer edges of the quilt. This placement is described by Linda Eaton, Curator of Textiles at Winterthur, as correlating with the placement of profile silhouettes in albums, studied by Anne Verplanck, that were compiled in the 1810s and 1820s by wealthy Orthodox members of Philadelphia's Quaker community.[9] The images in these albums, like the blocks of many single-pattern friendship quilts, were arranged according to the closeness of the individuals to the maker in an attempt "literally to bind together extended networks of kinship and friendship."[10]

The ability to discern patterns in the location of names on a quilt depends on being able to identify, in detail, who the people were, how they may have been related or associated, and why they were considered part of the quilt recipient's specific community. If information about such relationships has not been passed down by the family that originally owned the quilt, this identification process requires a significant amount of research—research that may not be fruitful if relevant records cannot be found, have been destroyed, or never existed. Since it takes time, effort, and a certain amount of luck to define the past relationships of people named on a quilt, deliberate patterns of name placement may go undetected.

Names on Philena's Quilt

Sufficient records exist about the people listed on Philena's quilt to understand their relationships to her and to each other and why their names are placed as they are. Most valuable were the records maintained in the nineteenth century by Quaker meetings that enable the researcher to determine family relationships, discern occasional breaches of appropriate behavior, and track the movements of Quaker families moving from one meeting location to another as they migrated west or simply moved about one region of the country. The other sources used to determine the relationships documented on Philena's quilt included the following:

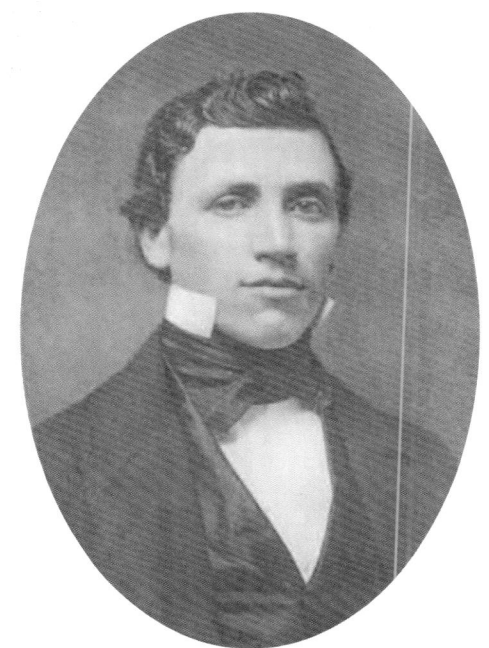

ILLUSTRATION 18. Chalkley J. Hambleton, c. 1887. Author's collection.

- the 1850 census for Columbiana County, which lists not only heads of households but also all people living within the household and on contiguous properties with names, ages, and places of birth;
- information on genealogical Web sites where descendants have documented their family trees;
- documents in archives and historical societies;
- obituaries printed in local papers;
- tombstone inscriptions;

- articles about early pioneers in the states of Ohio and Iowa;
- publications about the Underground Railroad in Pennsylvania, Ohio, and Iowa;
- county wills, probate records, deeds, and common pleas;
- nineteenth-century county and township maps displaying parcels of land with the names of landowners;
- and, luckily in this case, the luxury of a genealogical history of the Hambleton family in America written by Chalkley J. Hambleton in 1887 while family members named on the quilt were still alive.

35

Illustration 19 shows the result of color-coding the family names that appear on Philena's quilt. Red is for Hambleton, green for Cooper, sky blue for Hall, royal blue for Windle/Windell, gold for Clempson, orange for Ward, pale yellow for Mendenhall, and gray for Griffith and unknown. This diagramming technique makes it easy to detect groupings on a quilt's surface. Grouping by family name, however, does not always tell us about the relationships of the individuals involved. Only research can reveal these connections, especially for quilts made in small communities. The frequent intermarriage in the nineteenth century among a limited number of families within small communities makes it difficult to sort out cousins, aunts, and uncles from brothers and sisters, husbands and wives. The challenge is further exacerbated by a tradition of repeating the first names of family members generation after generation.

In the case of Philena's quilt, color-coding revealed a deliberate, symmetrical placement of family names and a subtle design feature that would not have been detected otherwise.

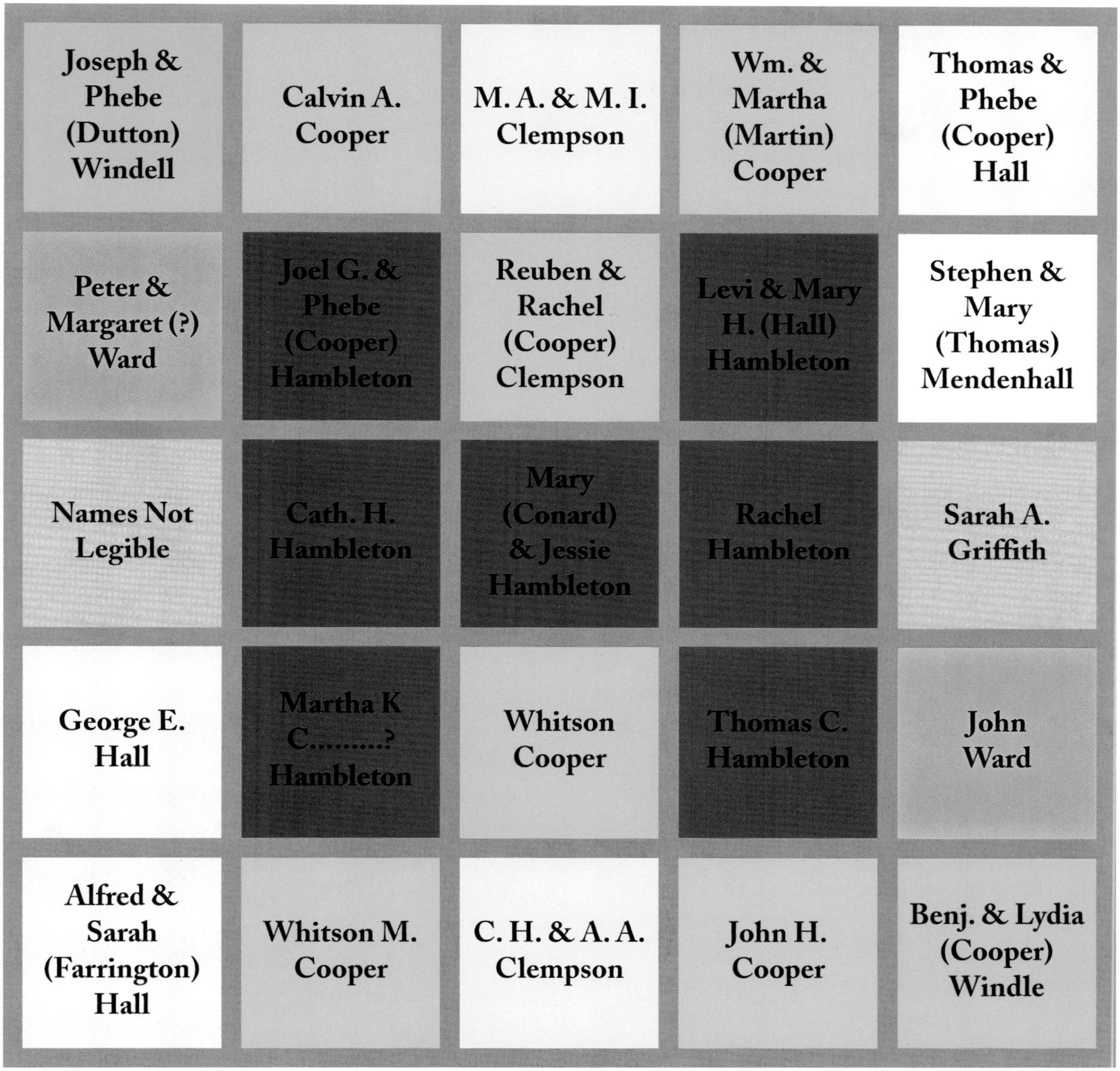

Joseph & Phebe (Dutton) Windell	Calvin A. Cooper	M. A. & M. I. Clempson	Wm. & Martha (Martin) Cooper	Thomas & Phebe (Cooper) Hall
Peter & Margaret (?) Ward	Joel G. & Phebe (Cooper) Hambleton	Reuben & Rachel (Cooper) Clempson	Levi & Mary H. (Hall) Hambleton	Stephen & Mary (Thomas) Mendenhall
Names Not Legible	Cath. H. Hambleton	Mary (Conard) & Jessie Hambleton	Rachel Hambleton	Sarah A. Griffith
George E. Hall	Martha K C..........? Hambleton	Whitson Cooper	Thomas C. Hambleton	John Ward
Alfred & Sarah (Farrington) Hall	Whitson M. Cooper	C. H. & A. A. Clempson	John H. Cooper	Benj. & Lydia (Cooper) Windle

ILLUSTRATION 19. Color-coded chart showing the placement of family names on Philena's quilt.

Family Groupings

The central three columns of quilt blocks contain the names of people who were Philena's most immediate family members. These core family members include her husband's six Hambleton brothers and sisters (two listed with spouses) and Mary (Conard) and Jesse, the wife and son of his first cousin, Joseph Hambleton, who lived in Cecil County, Maryland. Contiguous with these Hambleton blocks are six devoted to the Coopers. Whitson Cooper (deceased) and Rachel Bonner Erskine Cooper Clempson were Philena's parents as well as the parents of the four Cooper men named on the quilt, one listed with his wife Martha, and of Phebe A. Cooper, Philena's sister and the wife of Joel G. Hambleton. The two blocks dedicated to Clempson fill in the remaining spaces in the center column. These contain the initials of four girls who were the daughters of Rachel Cooper Clempson and Reuben Clempson, whom she married in 1837 after Whitson Cooper's death. These girls were Philena's half-sisters. Illustrations 20, 21, and 22 detail these relationships and illustrate the locations of their names.

The two outer columns of quilt blocks list the names of more distant relatives and close friends. Illustrations 23 through 27 display the placement of these names and describe the relationships of these people to Philena and to others named on the quilt.

A pattern of placement that clusters close family members in the center of the quilt and places others toward the outer edges generally follows that on the Quaker-made quilts mentioned earlier. However, Philena's quilt demonstrates a far more precise and deliberate positioning of names to both reflect family affiliations and provide a rigid symmetry in the placements.

Hidden Design

Philena's quilt is composed of single-pattern blocks all made with red and white fabric. The assembly of the blocks, themselves, reveals no particular design. When the names on the blocks were color-coded, however, a definite design element emerged. The most obvious is that the Hambleton names are placed to create a large "H" in the center of the quilt (refer to illustration 20). More subtle than the "H" are two possible "C"s formed by the blocks at top and bottom bearing the name Cooper (refer to illustration 21). These are followed by deliberate placements of the names of friends and other relatives along the left and right edges of the quilt to provide geometric symmetry (refer to illustrations 23 through 27). This symmetry breaks down only when George E. Hall's block is placed where one might expect to find a Mendenhall. Also, one cannot be sure that the symmetry would hold if the names eradicated by water damage on a block in the left-hand column of the quilt were visible rather than inferred. The strength of the overall placements does, however, indicate that the symmetrical placement of names on Philena's quilt was a planned and deliberate act.

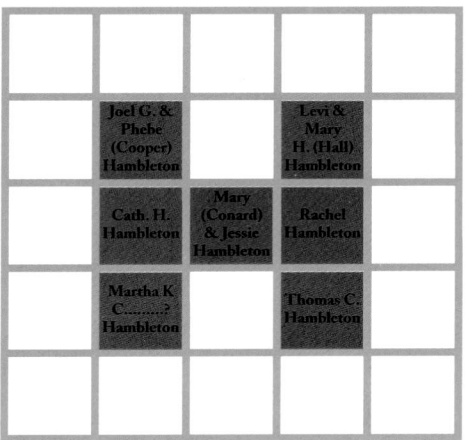

	Joel G. & Phebe (Cooper) Hambleton		Levi & Mary H. (Hall) Hambleton	
	Cath. H. Hambleton	Mary (Conard) & Jessie Hambleton	Rachel Hambleton	
	Martha K C.......? Hambleton		Thomas C. Hambleton	

ILLUSTRATION 20. Placements of the name Hambleton

Relationships:

All of the Hambletons were Philena's in-laws, the brothers and sisters of her husband, Osborn Hambleton, and, in the case of Mary (Conard) and Jesse, the wife and son of Osborn's cousin, Joseph Hambleton of Cecil County, Maryland.

Rachel Hambleton married Elisha Dutton, son of Joseph Dutton and the brother of Phebe Dutton Windell (Windle), in April 1853, after the quilt was made.

Phebe Cooper Hambleton, Joel G.'s wife, was Philena's sister. Their parents were Whitson and Rachel Bonner Erskine Cooper.

ILLUSTRATION 21. Placements of the name Cooper

Relationships:

Whitson Cooper and Rachel Bonner Erskine Cooper were Philena's parents. Rachel married Reuben Clempson (Clemson) in 1837, after Whitson's death.

Calvin A., William, Whitson M., and John H. Cooper were Philena's brothers.

Phebe A. Cooper, who married Joel G. Hambleton, was Philena's fifth sibling and only sister.

	Calvin A. Cooper		Wm. & Martha (Martin) Cooper	
		Reuben & Rachel (Cooper) Clempson		
		Whitson Cooper		
	Whitson M. Cooper		John H. Cooper	

ILLUSTRATION 22. Placements of the name Clempson (Clemson)

Relationships:

The initials of the children in these two squares are those of Philena's half-sisters, the daughters of her mother, Rachel, and Rachel's second husband, Reuben Clempson.

Mary A. and Maria Louisa, also referred to as Mariah, were placed on the upper square. Cecilia H. and Amelia A. were recorded on the bottom square.

		M. A. & M. I. Clempson		
		Reuben & Rachel (Cooper) Clempson		
		C. H. & A. A. Clempson		

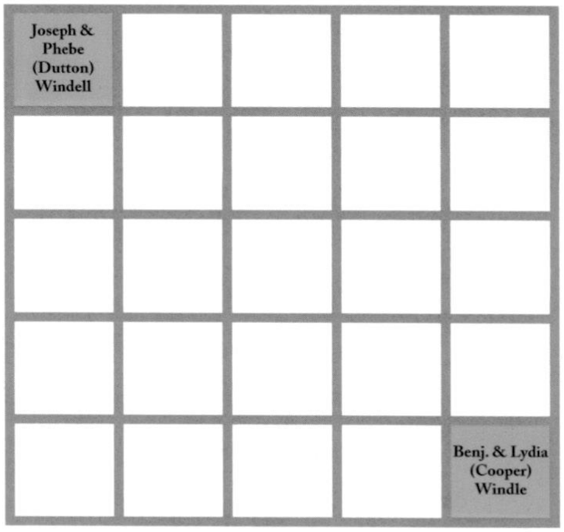

ILLUSTRATION 23. Placements of the name Windell (Windle)
Relationships:

Lydia Cooper Windle was Philena's aunt, the sister of her father, Whitson. Lydia married Benjamin Windle in 1822, the year Philena was born.

Joseph (J.) Windell (Windle) was the son of Benjamin Windle by his first wife, Orpha Jeffries. He became Philena's cousin by marriage. Joseph's wife, Phebe Dutton Windell, was the sister of Elisha Dutton who married Philena's sister-in-law, Rachel Hambleton, in April of 1853.

ILLUSTRATION 24. Placements of the name Ward
Relationships:

Peter Ward was a friend and neighbor of Philena and Osborn Hambleton in Butler Township. His first wife was Amy Galbreath. Two of Amy's cousins married two cousins of Osborn's father, Benjamin Hambleton.

John Ward was the youngest son of Peter and Amy Galbreath Ward. John lived with Levi and Mary Heston Hall Hambleton for a time, working as a clerk at their store in Marlboro, Stark County. Amy E. Ward, one of John's older sisters, was active in the New Garden Anti-Slavery Society with Philena and Osborn Hambleton, along with a number of local Galbreaths.

Peter and Amy Galbreath Ward's grandson, Peter Herbert Ward, married Joseph and Phebe Dutton Windell's daughter, Mary D. Windell.

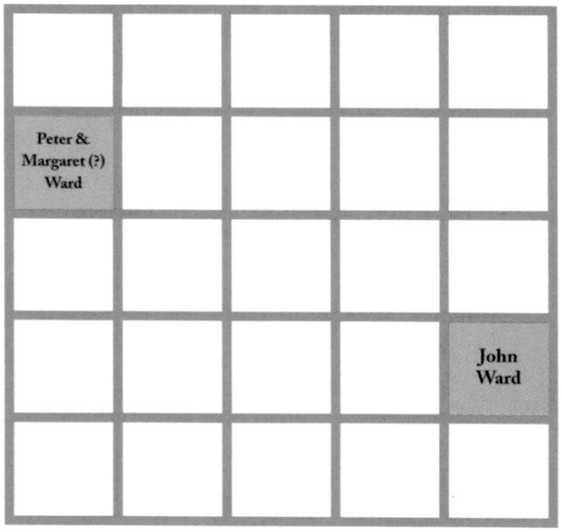

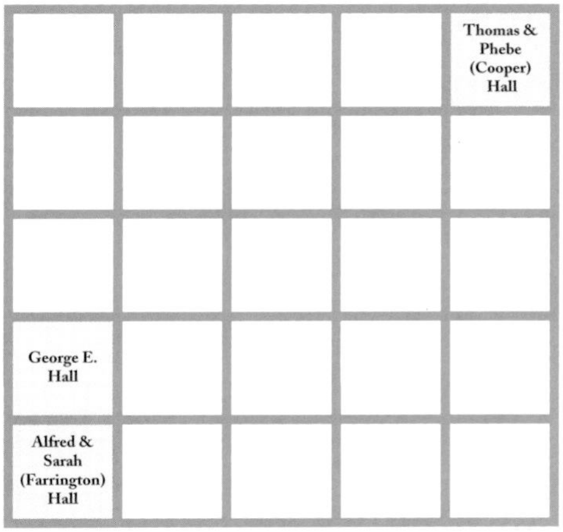

ILLUSTRATION 25. Placements of the name Hall
Relationships:

Phebe Cooper Hall was Philena's aunt, the sister of her father, Whitson, and of Philena's aunt, Lydia Cooper Windle.

Alfred Thomas Hall was Philena's cousin, the son of Thomas Vernon and Phebe Cooper Hall.

George E. Hall was the younger brother of Mary Heston Hall Hambleton, the wife of Levi Hambleton.

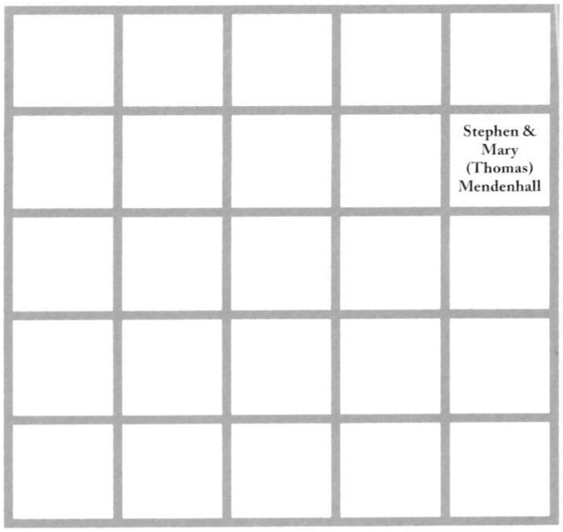

ILLUSTRATION 26. Placement of the name Mendenhall
Relationships:

Stephen D. Mendenhall's sister, Susan, was married to Jacob Dutton. Jacob's uncle, Joseph, was the father of Elisha Dutton, who married Rachel Hambleton in 1853, and Phebe Dutton, who was married to Joseph Windell.

Stephen and Mary Mendenhall operated a station on the Underground Railroad within eighteen miles of the station operated by Benjamin and Ann Hanna Hambleton on the property where Philena and Osborn lived.

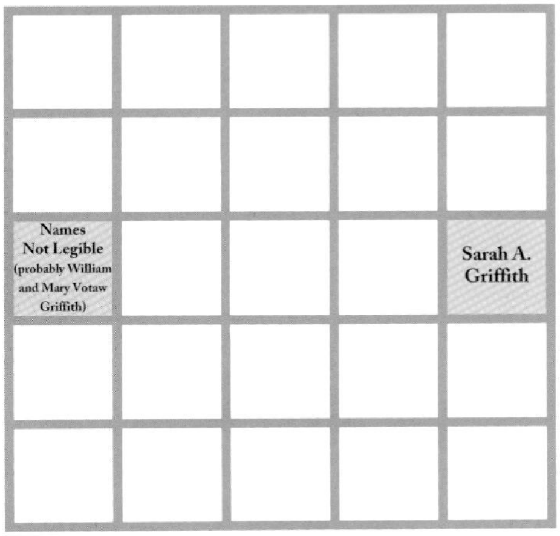

ILLUSTRATION 27. Placements of the name Griffith
Relationships:

Sarah A. Griffith was the daughter of William and Mary Votaw Griffith, both of whom were active in the New Garden Anti-Slavery Society with the Hambletons.

The square opposite Sarah's in the far left column is badly water-damaged and the names cannot be read, although the words New Garden and Columbiana County can be seen. Given the symmetry of other name placements, this square probably contained the names of Sarah's parents. The Griffiths were close friends and neighbors of Osborn and Philena Hambleton, and it is reasonable to expect that their names would be on the quilt along with that of their daughter.

Is the Quilt Really Philena's?

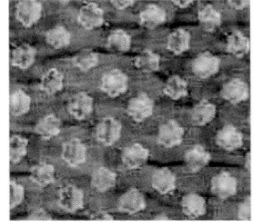

NINETEENTH-CENTURY SIGNATURE QUILTS, like their modern equivalents, were made for a purpose. Most signature quilts were made to acknowledge or commemorate a significant event in a person's life; to honor someone within the community; to affirm social, political, or religious beliefs; or to support an organization or cause as part of a fund-raising effort.

When quilts were made for a specific person, his or her name was often placed on the quilt with some notation that indicated whom the quilt was made for. This was the case when Ann Coppock's relatives and friends made and contributed blocks for her marriage quilt. If notations on a quilt do not indicate the quilt recipient, the names that are inscribed there and the dates, if any, can provide clues that may reveal the recipient's identity and why the quilt was made.

The names are the most important clues because they represent a community of people who were important in the life of the person for whom the quilt was made. These people are most often relatives, by blood or by marriage; close friends and neighbors; and community associates who share the beliefs and the social, religious, or political activities of the quilt recipient. Determining as many facts as possible about these people and their lives can lead to the one thing they all have in common—a relationship of some sort with the quilt recipient or with his or her family.

The frequent practice of grouping the names of close family members on nineteenth-century quilts can help one identify a core group of people who have a close relationship to the quilt recipient. This group likely represents the recipient's immediate family, so the task then becomes one of determining whether someone is missing who should have been included. The missing person (or persons) may be the one(s) for whom the quilt was made.

Once potential quilt recipients are identified, the next step is to discover as much about their lives as possible to determine whether they had a familial or a community relationship with each of the people named on the quilt. The stronger the relationships found, the more likely that person was the recipient of the quilt. If the quilt displays one or more dates within a limited span of time, those dates may indicate a life event, or purpose, for which the quilt was made. In the case of Ann Coppock's quilt, the dates 1846 and 1847 were displayed on a number of the quilt blocks. Ann married in 1847. In the case of Philena's quilt, the date 1853 appears on most blocks. The next year, she and her husband had moved to Iowa, leaving behind her community of relatives and friends in Ohio.

Philena's quilt does not bear her name, nor does it indicate in any way that it was made for her. Her identity as the quilt recipient was revealed by researching the lives of all of the people named on the quilt; examining the grouping and placement of their names; identifying people who could be expected to appear on the quilt but do not; and, of greatest importance, tracking the quilt to Tulsa, Oklahoma, and then to California through Philena's daughter, Angelina, and through Angelina's descendants.

The first step, however, was to determine whether the names placed on the center block of the quilt indicated that the quilt was made for them.

Mary and Jesse Hambleton on the Center Block

As mentioned earlier, the names of Mary and Jesse Hambleton appear on the block at the very center of the quilt. Mary is the only woman listed with a male on a single block whose name precedes that of the male. The center position with a woman's name listed first might indicate a recent marriage for which the quilt was made. But Mary, whose maiden name was Conard, had been married to Joseph Hambleton, a first cousin of the other Hambletons on the quilt, since 1831. Jesse was her son, and he was fourteen years old in 1853.[1] The fact that Mary's name precedes his is not remarkable since she was his mother. Further, census records and Chalkley J. Hambleton confirmed that Mary's and Jesse's permanent residence was in Cecil County, Maryland, not in Ohio. Mary was not a part of the local community of people named on the quilt.

Jane Bentley Kolter cites family reunions as one of the occasions when women got together to make friendship quilts that would commemorate the event and record those who participated. Sometimes a family member would bring the fabric to be used and encourage others to contribute blocks of their making as well.[2] The fact that Philena's quilt was made using what appear to be Turkey-red fabrics, so popular in Maryland and Pennsylvania at the time, might suggest that Mary brought fabric with her, initiated the quilt project while visiting relatives in Ohio, and returned to Maryland with the completed quilt. However, Turkey reds were then popular throughout all of the Mid-Atlantic states and the western states as well. Their use was not unique to Pennsylvania and Maryland.

The strongest arguments against Mary being the quilt recipient are the other names on the quilt. Although a Hambleton, she was one by marriage only and seems to have had no blood relationship to anyone on the quilt except her son, Jesse. Mary had no relationship to the Coopers, nor did she have known community ties to other Columbiana County residents named on the quilt. She had always lived in either Pennsylvania or Maryland. The only known evidence that she was ever in Ohio is the existence of her name on the quilt with the words Columbiana County, Ohio, and 1853 inscribed beneath it.

There is no way of knowing why the names of Mary and Jesse were placed at the center of the quilt. One might speculate that, since the locations of those named on the quilt appear to be where they were at the time the quilt was inscribed, Mary and Jesse were visiting Joseph's relatives in Ohio when the quilt was being made and that she was given a prominent place on the quilt to commemorate her visit. In any event, it is clear that the quilt was not made for her. If it had been, the names inscribed on it would have been quite different and would not have included those of Philena's parents and half-sisters—blood relatives of the wife of one of her husband's cousins.

Hambleton Couples Missing from the Core Family Grouping

The Hambleton names on the quilt reveal the unexpected absence of four critical family members —Osborn and Philena E. Cooper Hambleton and Osborn's parents, Benjamin and Ann Hanna Hambleton.

Osborn Hambleton was the oldest son of Benjamin and Ann and the only one of their living children not named on the quilt. Likewise, Philena E. Cooper Hambleton, daughter of Whitson Cooper and Rachel Bonner Erskine Cooper Clempson, is the only one of her parents' six children not named.

Every person on the quilt had a familial relationship or a regional association with the Hambleton and Cooper families. Osborn and Philena were both abolitionists who were active in their immediate community and regional area. They, along with

Osborn's father, Benjamin, and his sister, Rachel, were members of the New Garden Anti-Slavery Society. Their association with members of this society was a strong community tie and certainly explains, in part, the presence of the Wards and the Griffiths on the quilt. The Griffiths were also members of the New Garden Anti-Slavery Society, as was Peter Ward's daughter, Amy E. Ward. The Griffiths and the Wards were also neighbors, both families owning property near that of Benjamin Hambleton, where Osborn and Philena were living in 1850. As fellow antislavery sympathizers and farming neighbors, they might well be included on a quilt made to record community relationships of importance to Osborn and Philena or to Osborn's parents.

Of particular note is the presence of the names of both of Philena's parents on the quilt, even though one, her father, had passed away nearly twenty years before the quilt was made. The inclusion of Philena's parents, and not Osborn's, argues that the quilt was made for a member of the Cooper family. This conclusion is further supported by the fact that fourteen of the people named on the quilt were Philena's blood relatives. Only seven of those named were related to the Hambletons by blood even though there were many other Hambleton relatives in the area, including members of Ann Hanna Hambleton's prestigious family. If the absence of the names of Benjamin and Ann Hanna Hambleton signalled that the quilt had been made for one or both of them, the names of at least some of their siblings, and their oldest son, Osborn, would surely have been among those inscribed on the quilt. They were not. The reason that Benjamin and Ann Hanna Hambleton were not named on the

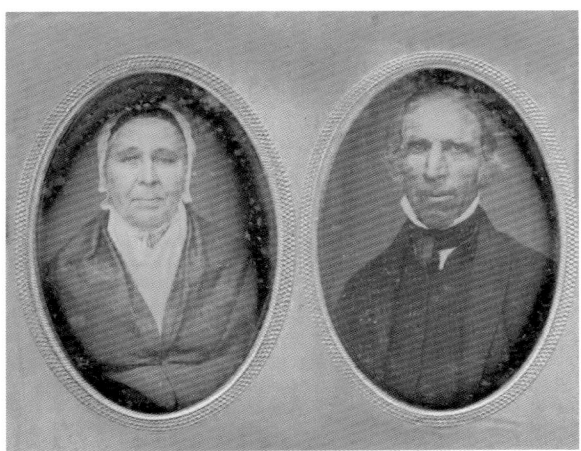

ILLUSTRATION 28. Benjamin Hambleton (March 15, 1789–April 25, 1865) and Ann Hanna Hambleton (July 30, 1797–March 10, 1867), Philena's father- and mother-in law, 1855. Photo courtesy of the Jerome Walker family.

quilt remains a mystery, but the evidence indicates it was not because the quilt was made for them.

Philena's quilt was inscribed between January 1 and April 7 of 1853.[3] Osborn and Philena were planning a move west, perhaps as early as the beginning of 1852, after the family mill Osborn managed was destroyed by fire. Iowa pioneer records indicate that the family relocated to Iowa in 1854. Both Osborn and his brother Levi bought land in Poweshiek County, Iowa, in 1855. Osborn built a steam mill that same year and Levi erected a large family dwelling at Forest Home, where the mill was located. Joel G. and Phebe A. Cooper Hambleton followed in 1857. The boys' parents, Benjamin and Ann Hanna Hambleton, who had remained behind in Columbiana County, moved to Iowa in 1865, eleven years after their oldest son and his family

left Ohio.[4] It must have been clear before and while the quilt was being made that major changes were under way—changes that would separate Philena and Osborn from most of their Ohio family members and sever their community ties in Columbiana County.

Philena and Osborn were the first to go, perhaps accompanied or shortly followed by Osborn's brother and sister-in-law Levi and Mary Heston Hall Hambleton. The absence of Osborn's and Philena's names on the quilt suggests that the quilt was made for Philena to document the loving community she was about to leave. Her name, and that of her husband, were not placed on the quilt that recorded what was soon to become their "old community." They and the quilt would be traveling west together. But is their movement west, plus the fact that Philena's name and that of her husband do not appear on the quilt when those of so many close relatives do, sufficient evidence that the quilt was made for Philena?

The Quilt's Journey from Iowa to Oklahoma and California

"It had always been in the family, and it came from an estate in Oklahoma." These were the words of the woman who placed the quilt on consignment in the antique store in Petaluma, California. If the quilt had been made for Philena, how did it physically end up in Oklahoma?

Osborn and Philena had two daughters, who were born in Ohio before the family left for Iowa. Their names were Angelina and Lorilla. In 1866, Angelina married Charles F. Craver in Sugar Creek

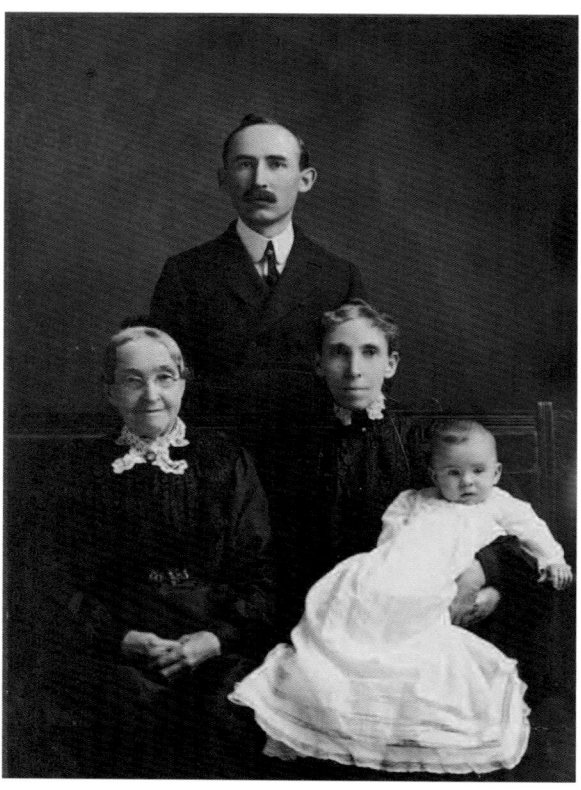

ILLUSTRATION 29. The quilt's path from Ohio to California represented by four generations. Philena Cooper Hambleton (seated left) brought it from Ohio to Iowa. Her daughter Angelina Hambleton Craver (holding baby) inherited the quilt when Philena died in Oklahoma. Angelina's son Arthur Hambleton Craver (standing) and his wife, Ada, inherited the quilt from Angelina. Ada moved from Oklahoma to California with the quilt after Arthur died and left it to her daughter, Florence Philena Craver Oberholtzer, the baby on Angelina's lap. Harvey, Illinois, 1903. Photo courtesy of the Jerome Walker family.

Township at Searsboro, the town where the family settled after moving to Iowa. Angelina and Charles subsequently had two sons, Arthur Hambleton Craver and Frank Steele Craver.[5] Lorilla, Angelina's younger sister, never married.

Obituaries provided by Pat Rowell for Philena, Lorilla, and Angelina state that they all passed away in Tulsa, Oklahoma. Lorilla died in 1914, while living with Angelina and Charles in Tulsa. Philena, too, was living in the Cravers' Tulsa home when she died in 1915. Angelina was the sole heir to Philena's estate.

The quilt's path from Ohio to Iowa to Oklahoma, and then to California can be traced only through Philena and her descendants. The path from Oklahoma to California was that followed by Ada Mertilla Craver, the widow of Angelina's older son, Arthur Hambleton Craver. Ada moved to California after Arthur died in 1944 to be near her oldest daughter, Florence Philena. Florence had married Kenneth Oberholtzer in Tulsa in 1928 and moved with him to California. In 1947, Ada went with Florence and Kenneth to Colorado, but they all returned to California after Kenneth retired in 1969, settling in Danville to the east of San Francisco Bay. Ada's second daughter, Ada Louise Craver Walker, was also then living in California with her husband, Robert Averill Walker.

Ada died on November 29, 1974, while living with Florence and her husband in Danville. Ada left the quilt and other belongings to Florence, her elder daughter and Philena's namesake. Florence had no children, and her husband predeceased her. When she, too, passed away at Danville in December 1995, she was taken back to Oklahoma and buried in the family plot in Tulsa. Her great-grandmother Philena's quilt became part of an estate sale in what is known locally as the East Bay and made its way north to the antique store in Petaluma where the author purchased it.[6]

Conclusion

The research conducted to determine the identity of the quilt recipient led most directly to Philena Cooper Hambleton. The conclusion that the quilt was made for her is based on the following:

- Philena had strong familial and community relationships with all of the people named on the quilt.
- Both of Philena's parents were named on the quilt, even though her father had passed away almost twenty years before the quilt was inscribed.

- Philena and her husband were missing from the family grouping displayed on the three center columns of the quilt.
- The impending departure of Philena and Osborn for Iowa corresponds with the dates placed on the quilt and is an event that would warrant the initiation and completion of a signature quilt that documented the community Philena was leaving behind.
- The deaths of both Philena and her daughter Angelina in Tulsa, Oklahoma, support the quilt dealer's assertion that the quilt had always been in the family and had come from an estate in Oklahoma.
- The quilt's path to California was traced through Philena's daughter and her descendants.

Philena's Story

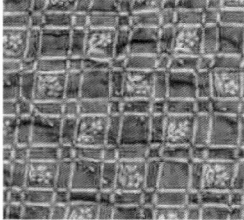

EVERY QUILT IS A POTENTIAL STORYTELLER. When provenance has been lost, a quilt may whisper only vaguely, revealing little about itself. Signature quilts, on the other hand, speak loudly with or without provenance. They are unique social and historic documents of the real-life communities their collective blocks represent. With patient research, the stories told by signature quilts can be revealed and their context reconstructed. The story of Philena and her community is the result of four and a half years of research into the lives of the people named on her quilt, as well as trips to Ohio and Iowa to visit the ground she walked. The story told here is Philena's. The stories revealed about all of the others will be told elsewhere.

The Early Years

Philena Evaline Cooper's life began in Clearfield County, Pennsylvania, on September 13, 1822.[1] Her father, Whitson Cooper, was born in 1792, the son of Quakers Calvin and Elizabeth Simcock Cooper of Chester County, Pennsylvania, devoted members of the Bradford Monthly Meeting.[2] Her mother was Rachel Bonner Erskine (Askey), the daughter of Robert and Mary "Polly" Evans Askey, a Presbyterian Scots-Irish couple who had homesteaded on the west branch of the Susquehanna River about three miles north of what was to become Curwensville.[3]

Whitson moved to Brady Township, Clearfield County, in 1820 after being disowned by the Bradford Monthly Meeting for having fathered an illegitimate child.[4] He met Rachel shortly after arriving there and becoming a teacher in a log-cabin school at Luthersburg. Whitson seems to have courted Rachel, and her family, convincingly and with charm. At sixteen years of age, Rachel married Whitson on March 27, 1821.[5]

Whitson and Rachel remained in Clearfield County through the time of the 1830 census, which found them living in or near Curwensville. By then, Philena had acquired a sister and two brothers:

Phebe, born May 6, 1824; Calvin A., born March 29, 1826; and William A., born June 17, 1828. Within the next five years, two more children were added to the family: John Hoyt, born August 4, 1831, and Whitson Milton, born May 2, 1835.[6]

The year of Whitson Milton's birth marked the beginning of drastic changes in the life of Philena, her mother, and her siblings. Philena's father had stopped teaching school by this time and had gone to work in the lumber business. An Iowa newspaper article written about Joel G. Hambleton and his wife, Philena's sister Phebe, later recalled that Phebe's father "was a lumberman and a raftsman and died while down the river at one time with a raft of lumber." He drowned on April 4, 1835.[7]

A letter written on July 4, 1904, by Nellie Reynolds Cranker described to her cousin what became of the family after Whitson's death. According to her, Rachel and Whitson were living on 160 acres that had been left to Rachel by her father, Robert Erskine. This property was confiscated by Whitson's creditors and, although the house was not taken, most of its furnishings were. Rachel was left with only a single bed and a few household belongings that were critical for survival. She was unable to support her children, some of whom were taken in by her Cooper relatives. Twelve-year-old Philena likely remained with her mother after Whitson's death to help Rachel earn money as a seamstress of men's clothing. Philena would also have been needed to assist with the care of her youngest brother, Whitson Milton, who was born just one month after Whitson's death and was named in his honor.[8]

An indication of the impact of Whitson's death on Philena's life is seen by the record of his death on the quilt she received eighteen years later. Rather than simply bearing his name, the block devoted to her father recalls the event itself. It poignantly reads, "Whitson Cooper Died in the Year 1835."

The majority of Whitson's family had remained in Pennsylvania, but by 1834 two of his married sisters, Phebe and Lydia, had moved to Columbiana County, Ohio, with their husbands, Thomas V. Hall and Benjamin Windle.[9] Thomas V. and Phebe Hall settled with their children in West Township near Lynchburg. Benjamin and Lydia Windle acquired property in Butler Township, as well as a family residence near Franklin Square in Salem Township.[10]

Whitson's sisters Lydia and Phebe probably shared the burden of caring for most of Whitson's children just after he died. Within two years, Rachel and the children who remained with her in Clearfield County had moved to Columbiana County to live with Whitson's oldest sister, Phebe, on the Hall's West Township property. It was here that Rachel most likely met Reuben Clemson (spelled Clempson on Philena's quilt) from Chester County, Pennsylvania. Reuben was a member of the Bradford Monthly Meeting—the meeting that had earlier disowned Whitson and which was also attended by Thomas V. and Phebe Cooper Hall before they relocated to Ohio. Reuben's occupation at this time is not known, but census entries from 1850, 1860, and 1870 indicate he was a postmaster, a retired wheelwright, and a laborer. Another record states that he had, at one time, taught school.

Rachel and Reuben were married in Columbiana County on April 25, 1837. Reuben, the son of James and Hannah Trego Clemson, was forty years old at the time and was condemned by the Bradford Monthly Meeting back in Pennsylvania for marrying

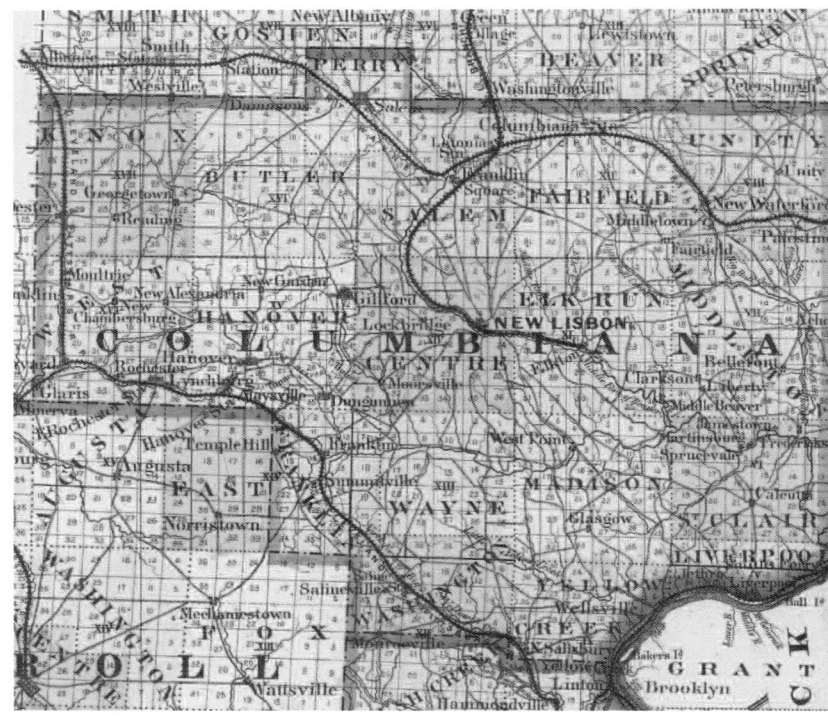

ILLUSTRATION 30. Map of Columbiana County from *Walling's Atlas of Ohio, Counties of Columbiana, Jefferson, Carroll and Harrison*, 1870.

out of the Quaker faith. His membership was later reinstated, and he received a certificate of transfer from Bradford to the Salem Monthly Meeting in Ohio, and then to the New Garden Monthly Meeting attended by the Hambletons.[11]

Philena was fourteen years old when her mother remarried. It is not known whether all of the Cooper children moved into the Clemson household at Lynchburg after the marriage. The Halls remained in West Township at least through 1841,[12] and some of Philena's brothers may have stayed with them to help on their farm. Philena and her twelve-year-old sister, Phebe, surely moved into the Clemson household with their mother. Not only were they young girls, they were needed there to help with the housework and watch over their

youngest brothers. These tasks undoubtedly became more burdensome when a series of half-sisters began to arrive in 1838 with the birth of Cecilia Hannah, Rachel's first daughter by Reuben. Cecilia was followed by Amelia Anna in 1840, Mary Adaline in 1842, and Maria Louisa in 1844.[13]

Insight into the daily lives of Philena and her mother after they moved to West Township is provided by the surviving letters of Anna Briggs Bentley, a member of the Sandy Spring Monthly Meeting. She and her family lived at Green Hill, within walking distance of Lynchburg and their neighbors, Thomas V. and Phebe Hall.

Anna and her husband, Joseph, moved to West Township from Maryland in 1826. Her letters to family back home date from 1826 into the 1880s,

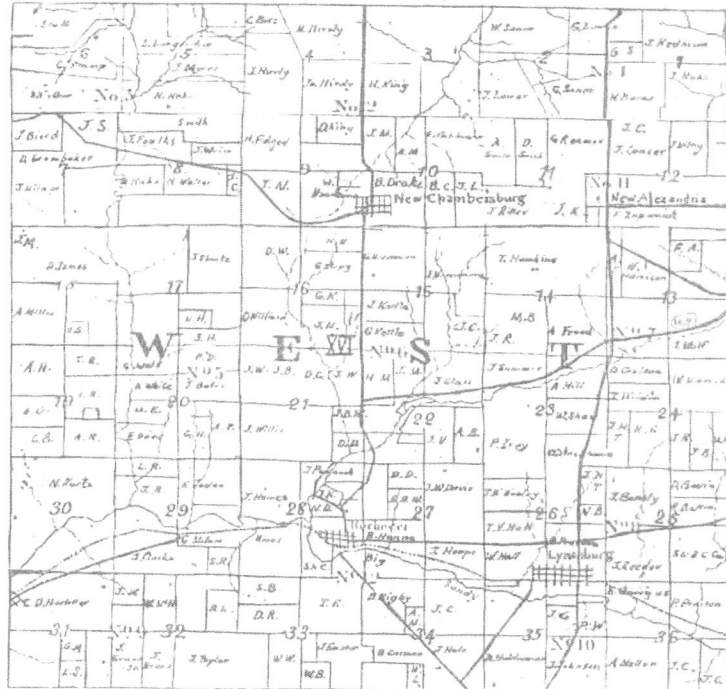

ILLUSTRATION 31. Map of West Township, Columbiana County, Ohio, in 1841, showing individual properties and the names of owners. The highlighted properties indicate the farms of Thomas and Phebe Cooper Hall, the farm of Joseph and Anna Briggs Bentley, and the town of Lynchburg, where Philena lived after her mother married Reuben Clempson. Courtesy of the Columbiana County chapter of the Ohio Genealogical Society.

and those written from 1837 through March 23, 1842, cover the time that Philena was still living with her mother in the Clemson household.[14]

Anna gave birth to her eleventh child in 1836, at age forty. Rachel, Philena's mother, was thirty-four when she had her seventh child in 1838, the first of four surviving children she would have by Reuben. Anna's letters to her family in Maryland detail the difficulties of continuing to give birth on the frontier as she grew older, far from the extended family that might otherwise have assisted in the care of her existing children. Her letters describe the extent to which she had to rely on her older daughters to take over household chores, gardening, and the care of her younger children while she nursed and tended her infants. Rachel was in a similar position,

and with the addition of each new child to the Clemson household, Philena and Phebe had to assume greater responsibilities in caring for the growing family.

The daily lives of Philena and Phebe, however, were not limited to chores and the care of family members. Quaker families traditionally educated their girls as well as their boys, and it is clear that both Philena and Phebe received some education at a primary school or, perhaps, at home. Their father, Whitson, had been a schoolteacher, and their stepfather, Reuben, reportedly also taught school. Both could have instructed the girls in reading and writing and may have taught them arithmetic skills as well. It is not known whether either girl attended secondary school.[15]

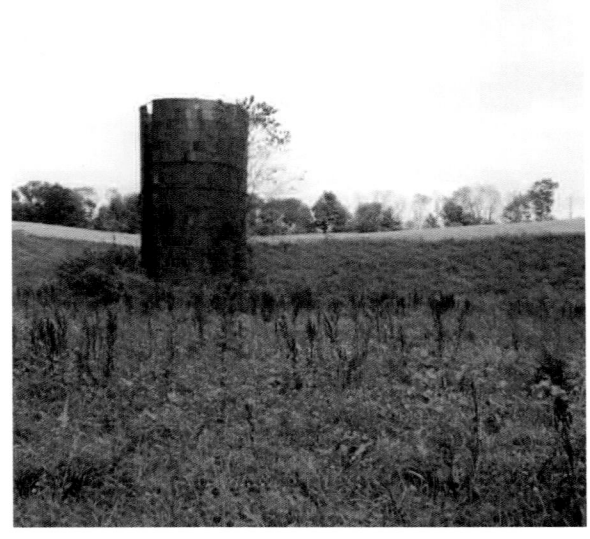

ILLUSTRATION 32. The remains of a silo on the Bentleys' Green Hill farm property. Date of silo unknown. No other structures appear on the property. Photo by author, 2004.

When Philena married Osborn Hambleton, she gained six brothers- and sisters-in-law: Rachel, then thirty-five years old; Levi, twenty-one; Catherine, nineteen; Joel G., seventeen; Thomas C., ten; and Martha K., eight. The names of each of these in-laws were inscribed on Philena's quilt in 1853.

Philena's mother- and father-in-law were both from notable families with origins in Chester County, Pennsylvania. Her mother-in-law, Ann Hanna Hambleton, was from a prestigious Quaker family living in the town of New Lisbon, about seven miles from the Hambleton property where Philena and Osborn were to live as man and wife. The Hanna family were related to President James Monroe through Ann's mother, Catherine Jones Hanna.[17] Ann's brother, Benjamin Hanna, was a major figure in the development of New Lisbon and the Sandy and Beaver Canal, a project that later failed due to financial conditions and changing times. The family, however, continued to be prominent in economic and political affairs. Benjamin Hanna's grandson, Marcus A. Hanna, later became an Ohio senator.

Philena's marriage not only gave her new relatives, it placed her in the middle of an abolitionist family with a long history of antislavery advocacy and action. Philena's father-in-law, Benjamin Hambleton, was a devoted supporter of the abolitionist cause, as were at least two of his brothers, Charles and Thomas, who remained in Chester County, Pennsylvania, after Benjamin relocated to Ohio.

Charles, Benjamin's youngest brother, was an important link in transporting fugitive slaves from

After coming to West Township, Philena and Phebe appear to have begun attending Quaker meetings. Although their mother, Rachel, was not of the Quaker faith, their father, Whitson, had been, as had their aunts, Phebe Hall and Lydia Windle prior to their marriages. Their stepfather, Reuben, attended the New Garden Monthly Meeting a few miles north of Lynchburg and it may have been here that the girls met their future husbands, the brothers Osborn and Joel G. Hambleton.

Philena was the first to marry. She left the Clemson household on March 24, 1842, when she and Osborn Hambleton were united in a civil ceremony.[16]

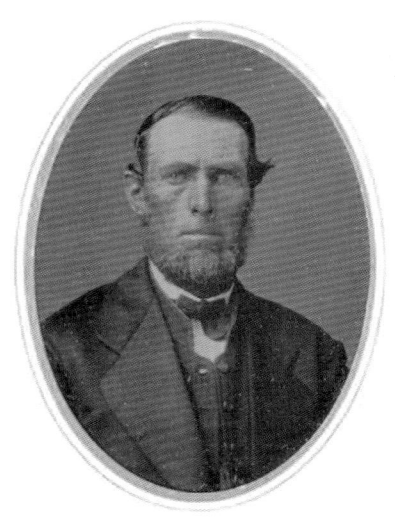 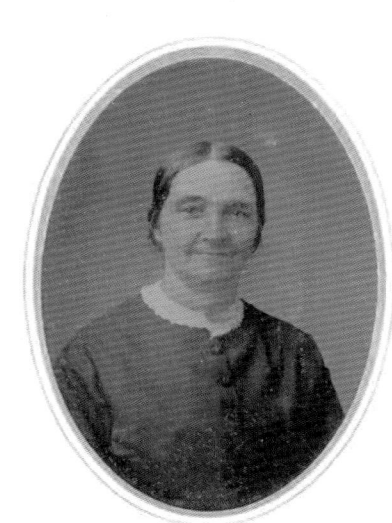

ILLUSTRATION 33. Osborn Hambleton (June 13, 1818– November 25, 1882) and Philena Cooper Hambleton (September 13, 1822–March 20, 1915). Date of photo unknown. Courtesy of the Jerome Walker family.

the borders of Maryland and Delaware to the Lancaster County town of Christiana, a free black community to the northeast of his home. The home he shared with his wife, Henrietta Simmons, was a station on the Underground Railroad and often hosted major figures of the antislavery movement, including Frederick Douglass, William Lloyd Garrison, Lucretia Mott, Sojourner Truth, and Harriet Tubman.[18]

Benjamin's brother Thomas and his wife, Alice Eliza Betts, also actively assisted fugitive slaves[19] and were among the founders of the Pennsylvania Yearly Meeting of Progressive Friends at Longwood in 1853, the year Philena's quilt was completed. This meeting was frequented by outspoken reformers from Philadelphia and elsewhere to debate and promote actions needed to address slavery, crime, war, women's rights, temperance, and other social and political issues.

Upon coming to Ohio in 1812, Benjamin first settled at Sprucevale in St. Clair Township, where he went into business with three of his cousins to form Hambleton and Company, an enterprise with a large farm, linseed oil and grist mills, and a retail store.[20] Benjamin probably met Ann Hanna while attending the Carmel Meeting of Friends in Middleton Township, five miles north of Sprucevale. It was there that Benjamin and Ann married on December 14, 1815, in a ceremony conducted by Clerk Nathan Heald.[21]

Benjamin and Ann moved to the west with five children in the summer of 1826,[22] settling on property in Butler Township about a mile north of the Hanover Township line. In 1834, the New Garden Anti-Slavery Society was founded at New Garden, a small hamlet about three and a half miles from the Hambleton home. The minutes from this meeting dated 1838–40 show that Benjamin, Osborn, and

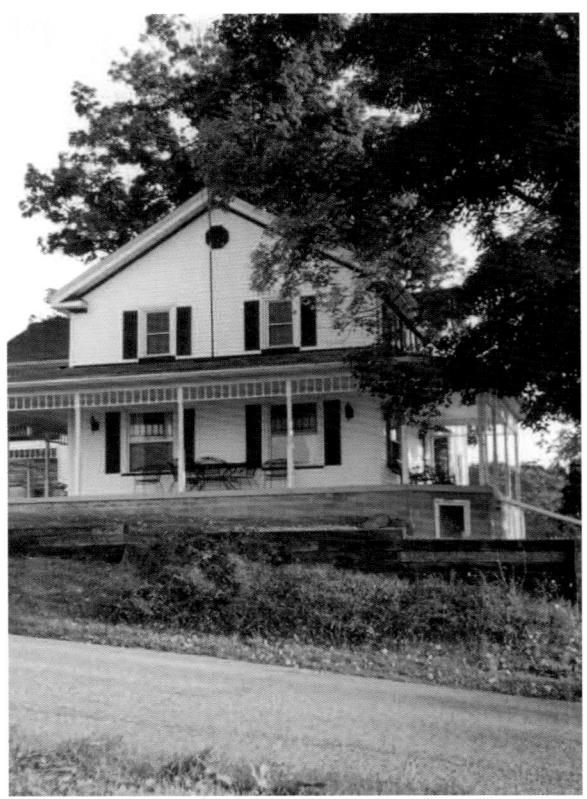

ILLUSTRATION 34. The home of Benjamin and Ann Hanna Hambleton, located on the corner of Butler Grange and Winona roads, Section 33, Butler Township, Columbiana County, Ohio. The original brick structure now has modern siding, and a large addition has been added to its south side. Photo by author, 2004.

Rachel Hambleton were active members of the society prior to Osborn's marriage to Philena.[23]

The house that became the Hambleton home in Butler Township still stands on the corner of Winona and Butler Grange roads. It is a brick house now covered with modern siding and displaying a modern addition to its southern side. This is the home that Philena entered when she married

Osborn in 1842—the home of her father-in-law, Benjamin Hambleton, described by Chalkley J. Hambleton as "a firm and active anti-slavery man, [who] assisted and harbored fugitive slaves in his own house when it was a dangerous business."[24]

Philena's new home in Butler Township was surrounded by rolling, green farmland. Like the land around it, the Hambleton property was devoted to farming, but it also boasted a mill, built by Benjamin Hambleton in 1830 and powered by water diverted from a stream on neighbor Samuel Grisell's property.[25] Osborn, after returning home from the Quaker Westtown Boarding School in Pennsylvania around 1835, assumed responsibility for the mill operations with his father. He eventually rented the mill from his father and became its sole manager/operator, providing him with sufficient income to marry Philena and begin a family of his own.[26] The first member of this new family was a daughter, Angelina, who was born on June 29, 1843.[27]

While Osborn ran the mill, Philena spent time tending her child, participating in the daily life of Osborn's family, and meeting the neighbors within her immediate community. These neighbors included Margaret and Peter Ward, who lived with their youngest son, John, on property they farmed just to the northwest across Winona Road. To the northeast was the residence of Joseph and Phebe Dutton Windle. William and Mary Votaw Griffith and their daughter Sarah lived a bit farther to the east on land that William farmed while also running a successful carpentry shop.[28] Butler Township property maps for the years 1841 and 1860 (illustrations 36 and 37) show the locations of these properties. The names of all of these neighbors appear on Philena's quilt.[29]

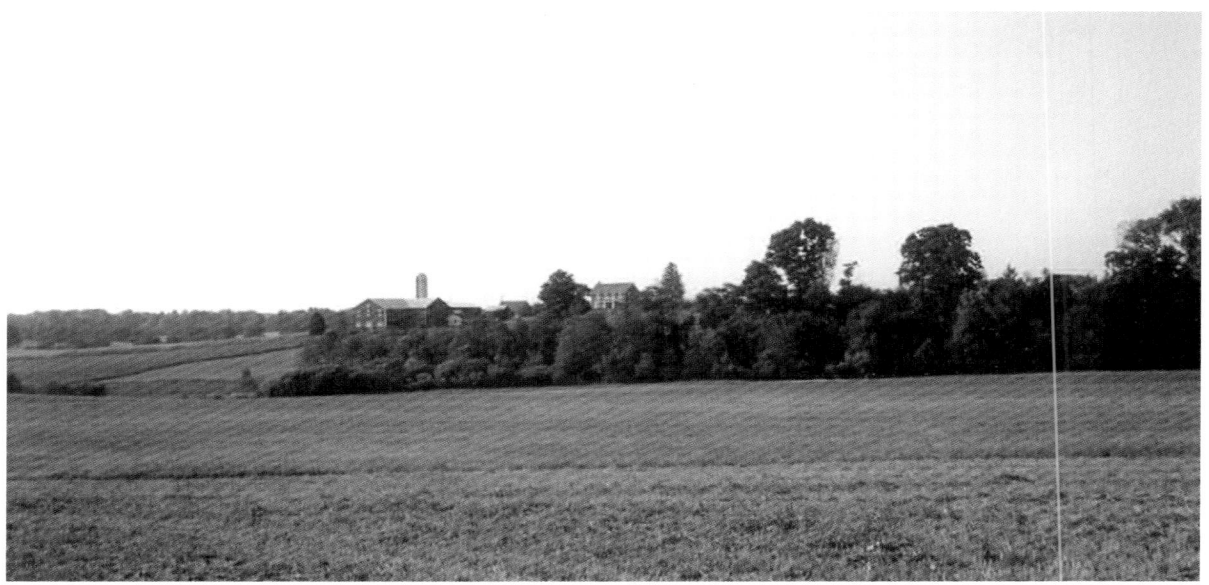

ILLUSTRATION 35. Section 29 of Butler Township, across the road and to the northwest of the Hambleton property at Butler Grange and Winona roads. Visible in the foreground is the former property of Peter Ward. The brick house on the hill belonged to William Galbreath, the father of Peter Ward's first wife, Amy Galbreath. William Galbreath purchased the northern half of the section about 1810, and his son-in-law, Peter, purchased the southern half. These combined properties measured one square mile at the time. Photo by author, 2004.

Philena's connection to some of her neighbors went beyond proximity. After marrying Osborn, Philena became a Hicksite member of the Religious Society of Friends. William and Mary Votaw Griffith were Hicksites, as were several of Philena's other nearby neighbors, including the Galbreaths and the Votaws. These particular neighbors were also active in the antislavery movement, which pervaded the lives of the Hambletons. Osborn had been a member of the local New Garden Anti-Slavery Society before marrying Philena, and both Philena and Osborn were members of the statewide Ohio Anti-Slavery Society after their marriage.

William and Mary Votaw Griffith, several members of the Galbreath family, and members of the Votaw family were also members of both societies.[30]

Religious ties and social commitment to the abolition of slavery, an unpopular cause even among some Quakers of the day, were connections that strongly bound Philena's community of friends after her marriage. The dangers inherent in hiding and transporting fugitive slaves, a federal offence punishable by imprisonment after the Fugitive Slave Act of 1850,[31] further strengthened the ties of those within the community who knew about or were engaged in such activity. Chalkley J. Hambleton

ILLUSTRATION 36. Map of Butler Township, Columbiana County, Ohio, in 1841, showing individual properties and the names of owners. The highlighted properties were those belonging to neighbors who were named on Philena's quilt: Peter and Margaret Ward; Benjamin and Lydia Cooper Windle; Benjamin Hambleton's (B. H.) sons and daughters; and Sarah Griffith and her parents, William and Mary Votaw Griffith. Courtesy of the Columbiana County chapter of the Ohio Genealogical Society.

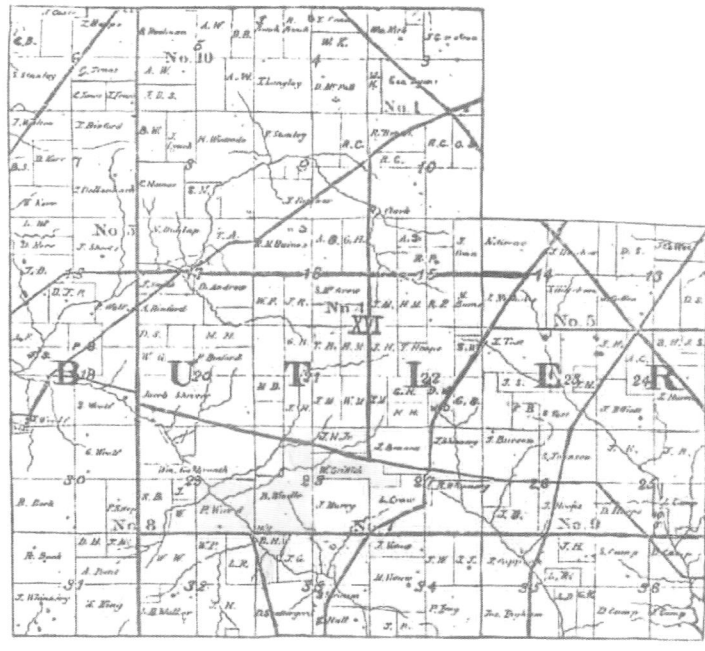

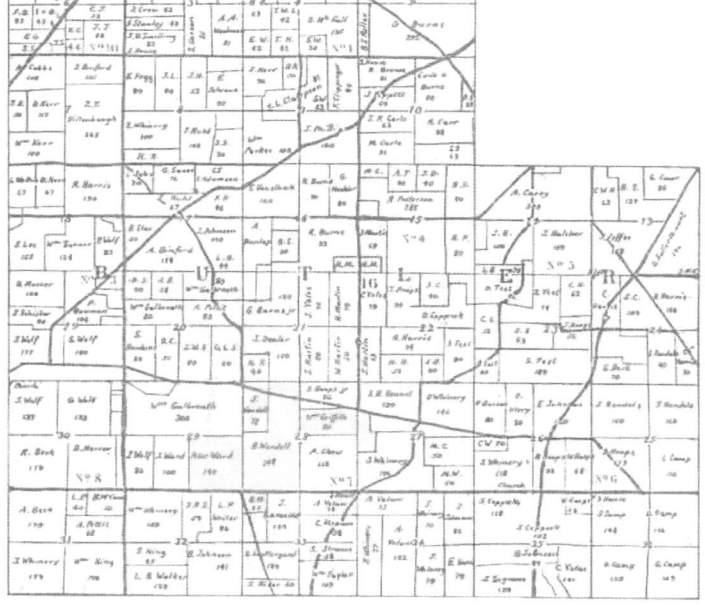

ILLUSTRATION 37. Property map of Butler Township, Columbiana County, Ohio, in 1860. The highlighted properties show that Joseph Windell (Windle), named on Philena's quilt with his wife, Phebe Dutton Windell, now owned property next to that of his father, Benjamin Windle. The Benjamin Hambleton property was reduced in size by 1860 and was sold to Joseph Windell when Benjamin and Ann Hanna Hambleton left Butler Township in 1864 to join their children in Iowa. Courtesy of the Columbiana County chapter of the Ohio Genealogical Society.

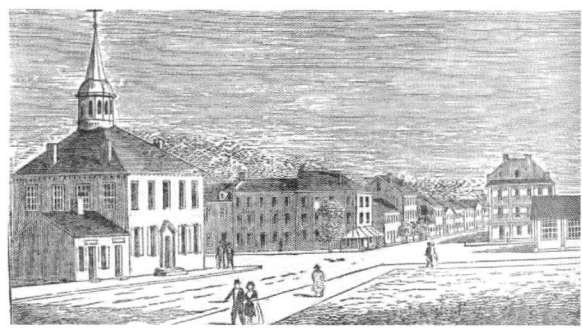

ILLUSTRATION 38. Illustration of the public square in New Lisbon, Henry Howe, 1846. From Henry Howe, *Historical Collections of Ohio*, volume 1 (Cincinnati: C. J. Krehbiel and Co., 1907), 438.

indicates that Benjamin Hambleton, Osborn's father, was engaged in this "dangerous business" on the property where Philena and Osborn lived. Osborn, given his antislavery sentiments, probably assisted in this effort. Both Benjamin and Osborn may have been transporting fugitives about eighteen miles northwest from the Hambleton home to Marlboro, Stark County, where Stephen D. and Mary Thomas Mendenhall, both of whom are named on Philena's quilt, operated another station on the Underground Railroad.[32]

Active support of the antislavery cause was found not just in Philena's immediate rural community but also in two nearby towns—New Lisbon and Salem.

Now called simply Lisbon, the town of New Lisbon was laid out in 1802 in Centre Township and became the county seat shortly after Columbiana County was formed. By the mid-nineteenth century, New Lisbon had three newspaper printing offices, seven churches of various denominations, including the Religious Society of Friends, two woolen factories, a variety of mercantile stores, two foundries, two flouring mills, and eighteen hundred residents.[33] These residents included Philena's in-laws, the Hanna family.

New Lisbon was a center of commerce and industry and an urban town where national and regional social-action and political issues were debated, publicized, and supported or opposed. Charles Osborn's antislavery paper, *The Philanthropist*, was popular in New Lisbon, and its local agent in 1817 was Benjamin Hanna, Philena's uncle by marriage.

New Lisbon became, in 1826, the first place in Columbiana County to hold a public meeting in support of the antislavery cause. The Columbiana Abolition Society was established there the next year, quickly gaining a membership of more than five hundred. In 1832, also in New Lisbon, John Frost published the first issue of the *Aurora*, a paper that would later vigorously oppose slavery.[34]

New Lisbon was a natural venue for speakers on the antislavery lecture tour and was one of the places visited by Quaker abolitionist Abby Kelley in 1845. She was invited to speak at the three-day convention of the Western Anti-Slavery Society that convened there on June 4. Approximately five hundred men and women crowded into New Lisbon's Disciples' Church to hear her, a portion of the crowd spilling out into the streets. Most of her listeners were Quakers, and most likely Philena, Osborn, and his parents, as well as other members of the New Garden Anti-Slavery Society, were in attendance. The audience liked what they heard and agreed to establish a regional antislavery newspaper, the *Anti-Slavery Bugle*, that would eventually be based in Salem.[35]

An even greater center of antislavery sentiment was the town of Salem, six miles to the northeast of

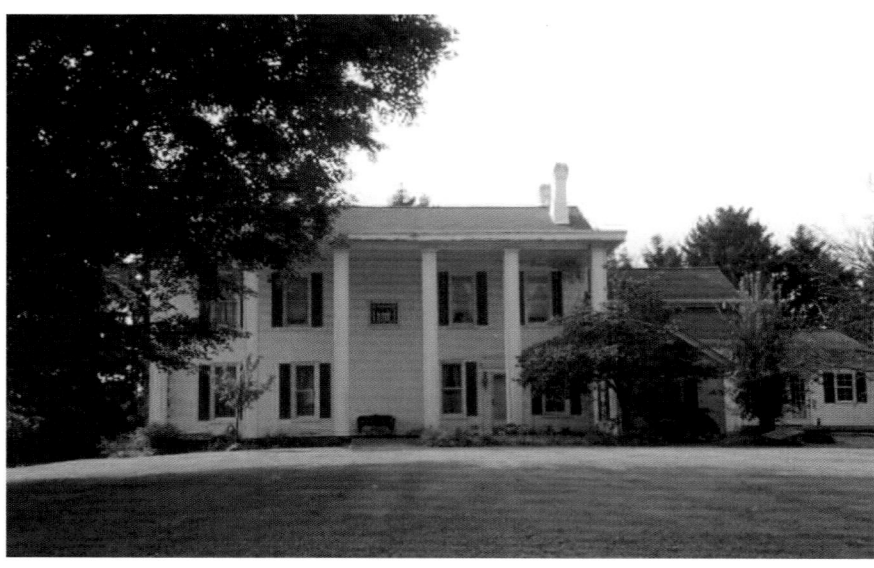

ILLUSTRATION 39. Advertisement listing Benjamin Hanna as one of the agents for Charles Osborn's antislavery paper, *The Philanthropist*. Collection of the Ohio Historical Society, Columbus, Ohio.

ILLUSTRATION 39. Advertisement listing Benjamin Hanna as one of the agents for Charles Osborn's antislavery paper, *The Philanthropist*. Collection of the Ohio Historical Society, Columbus, Ohio.

733

The Philanthropist.

Published Weekly

By Charles Osborn.

MOUNT PLEASANT,—OHIO.

SIXTH-DAY, NINTH MONTH 19th.

AGENTS FOR THE PHILAN-
THROPIST.

The following persons will please receive monies and subscriptions for the Philanthropist.

OHIO.

Smithfield—Wm. Blackstone.
Flushing—Amos Garretson.
Belmont—Joseph Wright.
Zanesville—Jesse Gause.
St. Clairsville—Benjamin Lundy.
Barnesville—Camm Thomas.
New-Lisbon—Benjamin Hanna.
Fairfield—William Heald.
Salem—John Street.
Richmond—A. Farquahar.
Cincinnati—Jesse Embree.

ILLUSTRATION 40. Benjamin Hanna's residence, New Lisbon, Columbiana County, Ohio. Photo by author, 2004.

the Hambleton home. The city was founded in 1806 by Quakers Zadok Street and John Straugham and became home to large numbers of Quakers from the states of Pennsylvania, New Jersey, Maryland, and Virginia. Most of these Friends were sympathetic to the antislavery cause, but there were also many in the area who opposed their views. Churches and public buildings eventually became off-limits for controversial antislavery meetings, and known abolitionists were frequently harassed and physically assaulted for the views they held. Even so, Salem's small antislavery group was one of the most active in Columbiana County, and many of the country's best-known abolitionist speakers passed through Salem, a bustling town of about thirteen hundred people by 1846.[36] Over time, Salem hosted several abolitionist events such as the antislavery convention held there in May 1847. Anna Briggs Bentley attended the event and described her impressions in a letter to her mother.

On 7th day 5th there was a great *antislavery* convention held there [Salem]. An immense and beautiful tent which cost 300 dollars (a present from Cousin Saml Brooke to the Society) was erected on an eminence. It is capable of holding 5000, but it could not anything like hold the vast multitude that poured forth from hill, and glen, city and cabin, from far and near. A raised platform held the speakers, who were William Lloyd Garrison—a most noble-looking man; I never saw such a head, all the moral and intellectual organs are very

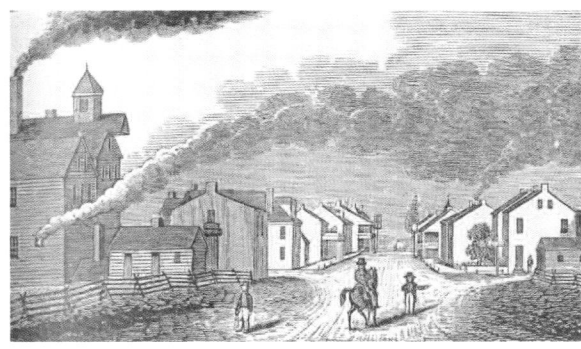

ILLUSTRATION 41. Illustration of the eastern entrance to Salem, Henry Howe, 1846. From Henry Howe, *Historical Collections of Ohio*, volume 1 (Cincinnati: C. J. Krehbiel and Co., 1907), 449.

large, benevolence and firmness enormous—Frederick Douglass, the celebrated fugitive from slavery—his master was Thomas Auld of Baltimore; he escaped 9 years since, is now 29 years of age. I wish you could see and hear him, he is the *perfect, polished* gentle*man* in his appearance and manners, his language forcible, entirely correct, elloquent [*sic*], touchingly so, and all his gestures so appropriate, natural and graceful I do not wonder that he can enchain the attention of assembled thousands. By his side sat Lucretia Mott; another very

talented, highly educated young gentleman, a Dr Peek of Pittsburgh—he is the colour of Jacob Hardesty—several others, but those I mention were Lions. A celebrated family of singers, a father and his two daughters (thier [*sic*] names Cowles), sat on the platform and sang. Oh, such singing. Douglass and Peek sang with them. It was the first meeting of the kind I ever was at, and I was highly delighted and think any of you would have been too, even Bro William Henry Farquhar, for there in our own free state we dare to avow our loathing of the foul plague spot on our country's glory.[37]

A gathering of national antislavery speakers such as this was not to be missed by those in the region who supported the cause. A turnout of over five thousand in a town of about thirteen hundred residents, as reported by Anna, demonstrates the importance placed on both the speakers and the issue of slavery in the immediate area. We cannot know whether Philena and Osborn were among those assembled that day, but it seems likely, given their involvement in the antislavery movement. If Philena was not there, it was because she had given birth to a second daughter, Lorilla, just seventeen days

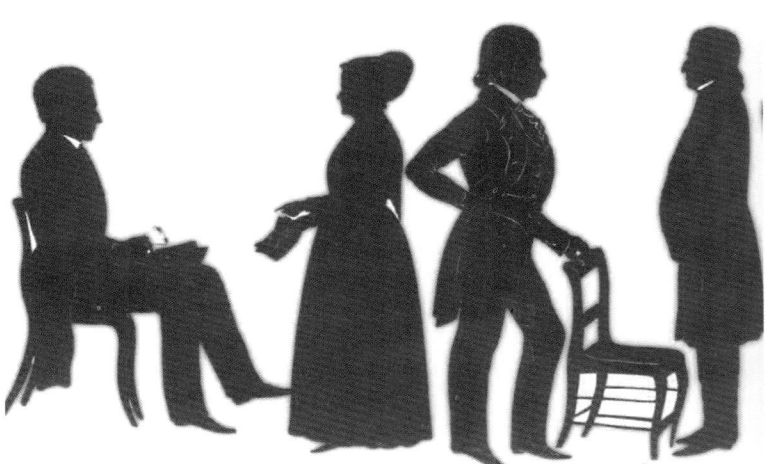

ILLUSTRATION 42. Page from an album of duplicate silhouettes made by August Edouart of Quaker subjects. Philadelphia, 1843. The silhouettes are those of abolitionists James Mott and his wife Lucretia Mott, who was a speaker at the antislavery convention held in Salem, Ohio, in 1847. The other silhouettes are those of Harry D. Landis and Elias Hicks, the Quaker reformer whose views resulted in the schism of 1827 that separated Orthodox Friends from Hicksite Friends. Collection of the Friends Historical Library of Swarthmore College.

before the event.[38] If she stayed home to tend and nurse the child that day, she would probably have regretted missing an opportunity to meet with neighbors and fellow abolitionists at a significant event that affirmed and strengthened the bonds of her community.

Three years later, at the time of the 1850 Columbiana County census, Angelina was seven and Lorilla was three. Osborn was a miller running the Hambleton mill, and Philena's youngest brother, Whitson Milton Cooper, was living with them on the Hambleton property. Whitson Milton was fifteen years old by then and was listed in the census as a laborer. He was certainly old enough to be working in the mill with Osborn, and he may also have helped Osborn's father, Benjamin, on the farm.

Shortly after 1850, the Hambleton mill was destroyed by fire.[39] Rather than rebuild in Butler Township, Osborn appears to have decided to build a new mill farther west in new territory. Thomas V. and Phebe Cooper Hall, Philena's aunt and uncle, had moved to Iowa from West Township prior to 1853.[40] They may have encouraged Osborn and Philena to come to Iowa, where land was fertile, inexpensive, and just opening for settlement. Whether encouraged by their relatives in Iowa or not, Osborn and Philena decided to move there. Their decision may have been discussed at length within the immediate family because Osborn's brother and sister-in-law, Levi and Mary Heston Hall Hambleton, decided to go as well. Their planned departure for Iowa appears to have inspired the quilt that was made for Philena in the months prior to its completion in 1853.

The quilting itself could have taken place at the Hambleton home in Butler Township. It was winter, and the activity would have been held indoors, accompanied by a meal for those who participated. One of Anna Briggs Bentley's letters described a similar event at Green Hill twenty-five years earlier that may give an indication of nineteenth-century quilting bee preparations and the food that would have been served at that time of year in Columbiana County: "Seth made me a nice pr of frames and I got it ready and 2nd day we had 22 women and 20 men . . . Allice Jackson helped with the baking and house cleaning . . . For dinner we had a turkey, 3 fowls, 3 quarters of a small veal, a nice peice [*sic*] of corned beef, potatoes, turnips, cold slaw, parsnips, pickled cucumbers and beets for supper and excellent green apple pies, peach and green apple sauce, real coffee, tea, rolls, light bread, pickles, fruits stewed, and relishes of cold meat left at dinner, pie, &c."[41]

Hopefully, Philena's sewing party was more productive than Anna's. Anna went on to report that she was totally exhausted from the effort and that not much sewing was done.

A New Land, A New Home

Osborn and Levi traveled to Iowa in 1854 to determine where they wanted to settle. By 1855, Osborn, Philena, their daughters, the quilt, and Levi and Mary Heston Hall Hambleton had relocated to Poweshiek County, Iowa, during a time of massive migration into the state. Officially formed as a state in December 1846, Iowa had a population of 192,214 in 1850 and had grown to 325,202 by the time the Hambletons arrived.[42]

Levi officially settled land that year which he laid out and platted as a small town. His wife, Mary, named the town Forest Home. It was located in what, due to Levi's later efforts, would become Union Township. Here he built brick kilns with workers he brought with him from Ohio and erected a large brick residence for his family and a wooden building to house his mercantile business.[43]

By early 1855, Osborn had purchased land for a house and farm near Searsboro in nearby Sugar Creek Township, Poweshiek County, and had erected a steam saw mill at Forest Home. According to a newspaper account of the Hambleton family that appeared years later in the *Montezuma Weekly Republican*, Osborn shipped the engine and boiler from the Ohio mill by water to the town of Keokuk and then hauled them to Forest Home by team.

Nothing remains of Osborn's mill at Forest Home, but the house that he and Philena built on their farmland still stands on what is now 60th Street to the east of Searsboro. The house is currently owned by Tassy Aldridge Guthrie, whose deed includes documentation of the original land purchase executed between the United States government and Osborn Hambleton. It cites an original entry date of March 10, 1855, conveying a section of forty acres. Today the farmhouse has modern siding and a few added features, but the land is intact and is still being farmed.

In 1857, Osborn's brother Joel G. and Philena's sister Phebe also packed up and moved to Iowa. They traveled by train to Iowa City and then made their way to Poweshiek County by horse and buggy. Joel took up farming near Searsboro to support Phebe and their two sons, Orlando and Linden B.[44] One can only imagine the joy felt by the two sisters at being reunited. Osborn, too, must have relished having two of his brothers in the immediate vicinity.

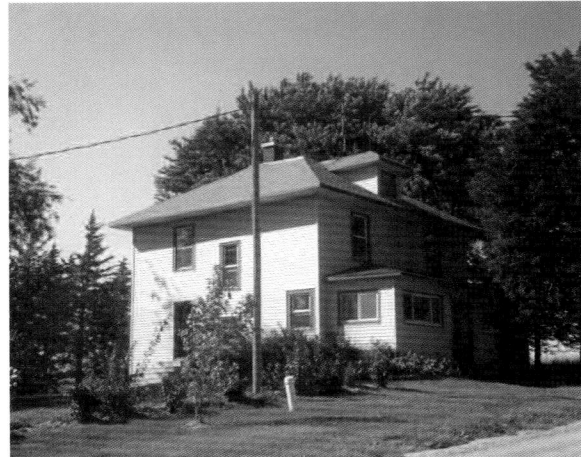

Illustration 43. The house that Osborn and Philena Cooper Hambleton built outside Searsboro, Poweshiek County, Iowa, in 1855. The house sits on the original forty acres purchased by Osborn from the United States government. The house has been somewhat modified over the years but retains its original core structure and basement area. Photo by author, 2004.

Osborn operated the mill at Forest Home for about three years before it burned down and he retired to his land in the spring of 1858. His decision not to reopen the mill and to take up full-time farming may have resulted from an accident at the mill or elsewhere. An 1880 biographical sketch of Osborn as a Poweshiek County pioneer states that he had only one arm.[45]

Osborn was admired throughout the area for the condition of his farm and his farming activity. His biographical sketch states, "His farm is a model of neatness, good fences and good buildings, and everything kept in good repair. He has his farm well stocked with horses, hogs and cattle, and has a portion of his farm seeded to grass, and has a good bearing orchard." The author of the sketch also

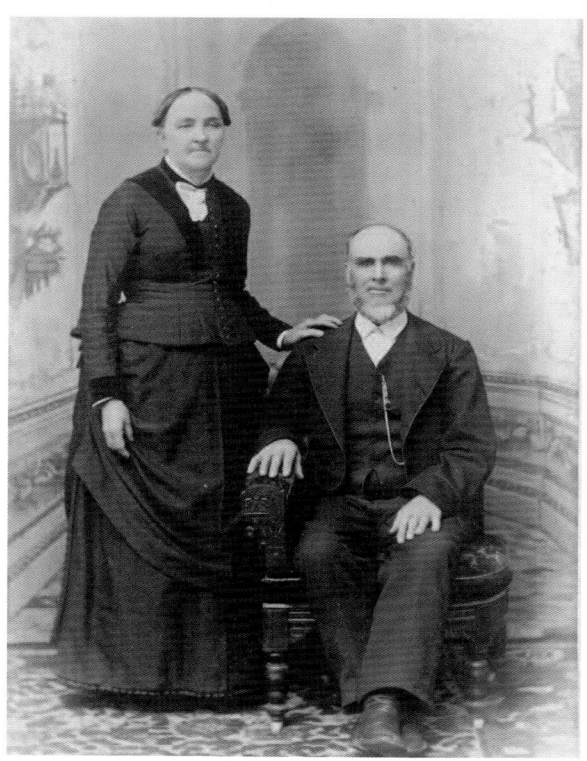

described Philena as "a woman of intelligence and fine taste and a most excellent housekeeper."

But not everyone in their Iowa community thought so highly of Osborn and Philena. They had carried their antislavery sentiments with them from Ohio to Iowa, and, by 1858, Osborn had established and was president of the Forest Home Anti-Slavery Society. Philena was a member of its executive committee. The minutes of the first meeting of this society, published in the *Montezuma Weekly Republican* on October 28, 1858, demonstrated its somewhat radical stance—a stance that even condemned the U.S. Constitution as a "nefarious and Heaven daring Compact" that sanctioned and encouraged slavery.

ILLUSTRATION 44. Joel Garretson Hambleton (September 16, 1824–April 9, 1912) and Phebe Cooper Hambleton (May 6, 1824–January 4, 1915). Date unknown. Photo courtesy of the Jerome Walker family.

Such bold proclamations, published for all to see, would certainly enrage members of the local populace who did not hold similar views. Evidently this was the case, for Osborn was further described in the biographical sketch previously mentioned as being a "man of very decided opinions of his own, and during the early excitement in regard to human slavery in this country he adopted the sentiments of the Abolition party, and suffered many indignities at the hands of some of his neighbors who held different opinions."

Joel G. and Phebe decided to settle permanently near Searsboro and, in 1864, bought ninety-five acres near Osborn's property in Sugar Creek Township, eventually adding another two hundred acres to this land and an additional residence on the northern outskirts of Searsboro after the town was laid out in 1871. They opened a lumber business soon after and also sold grain.[46] Joel became a prominent citizen of Searsboro over the years. He was elected

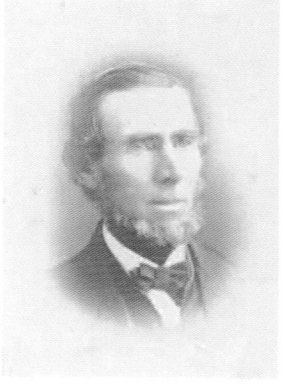

ILLUSTRATION 45. Osborn Hambleton. Date unknown but probably taken in Iowa after 1855. Photo courtesy of the Jerome Walker family.

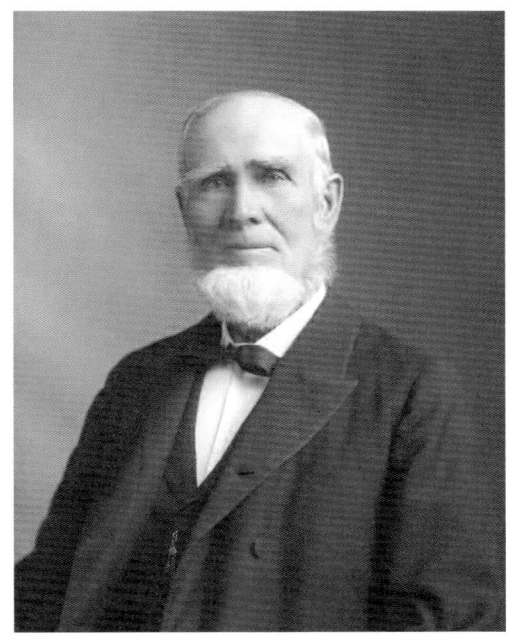

ILLUSTRATION 46. Joel Garretson Hambleton in 1904 at age eighty. Photo courtesy of the Jerome Walker family.

postmaster of the town in 1871 and served in this capacity until 1885. The post office itself was in a store that Joel and Phebe owned where coal, books, flour, and other goods were sold. Joel twice served as the town's mayor, became a member of Searsboro's Board of Supervisors, and also served as the town's school treasurer for fifteen years.[47] His active civic life was testimony to the esteem in which both he and Phebe were held throughout their lives in Searsboro, where they developed a large number of adoring friends.[48]

Meanwhile, Levi and Mary Heston Hall Hambleton suffered a fire in 1856 that destroyed their store in Forest Home and spent the next couple of years farming and improving property in the area. In 1871, Levi decided to reopen his mercantile business in Oskaloosa, several miles south in Mahaska County, where he would have access to the railroad for transporting goods. He set up shop on Oskaloosa's town square, but this business also burned to the ground. Undaunted, Levi reopened in the newly built brick Phoenix Block on the square's southeast corner. He later organized the Central Iowa Loan and Trust Company and became a noted businessman, civic leader, and cofounder of Penn College in Oskaloosa.[49] One of his sons Albert F. N. Hambleton carried on Levi's tradition as a successful businessman and civic leader.[50]

While Levi pursued his business interests, his wife Mary raised their children and participated in the community life of Oskaloosa. She was a devout Quaker, an abolitionist, and a dedicated member of the Woman's Temperance Crusade.[51] The national Woman's Christian Temperance Union (WCTU), established in 1874, grew out of the crusade and was

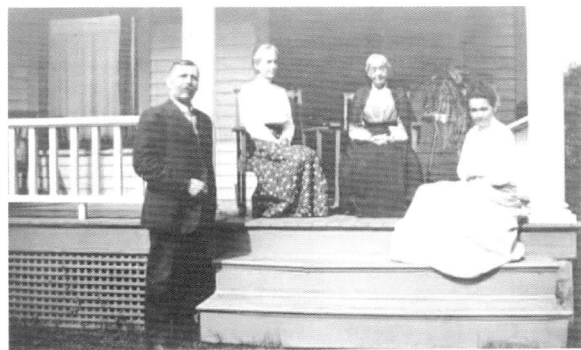

ILLUSTRATION 47. Levi Hambleton's son, Albert F. N. Hambleton, his wife, Josepha (Josie) Roberts Hambleton, Philena Cooper Hambleton, and Philena's youngest daughter, Lorilla. Date unknown, but taken prior to Lorilla's death in 1914. Photo courtesy of the Jerome Walker family.

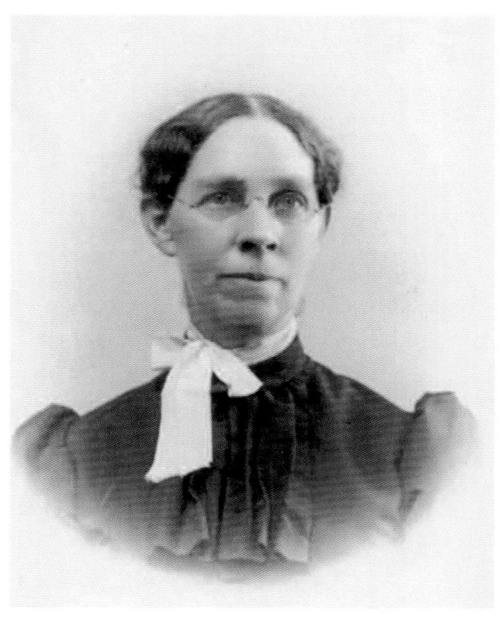

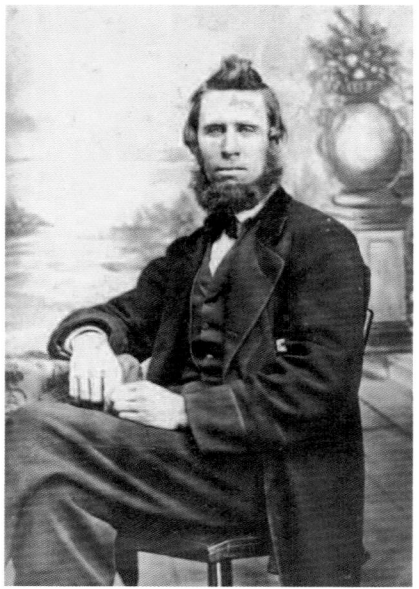

ILLUSTRATION 48. Philena's sister-in-law Martha K. Hambleton Craver (August 8, 1833–January 19, 1923), called Mattie by the family. Date unknown; probably late nineteenth century. Photo courtesy of the Jerome Walker family.

ILLUSTRATION 49. Philena's brother-in-law Thomas Clarkson Hambleton (June 30, 1831–October 2, 1903). Date unknown. Photo courtesy of the Jerome Walker family.

a major force in condemning the consumption and sale of alcohol and the plight of women subjected to rough treatment by drunken husbands.

Even though Levi and Mary moved farther away, there were many occasions for the Hambletons to visit one another and gather for family events. These gatherings had increased in size as additional members of Osborn's family moved to Iowa. Osborn's youngest sister, Martha K., had joined the family sometime prior to 1861, probably staying with Joel G. and Phebe until she married Henry Craver in August of that year.[52] Osborn's parents, Benjamin and Ann Hanna Hambleton, sold their house and property to neighbor Joseph J. Windle in 1864 and moved to Iowa to join their children.[53] Osborn's youngest brother, Thomas Clarkson, and his wife Emily Morlan also spent some time in Iowa while Thomas was teaching school in Oskaloosa in 1877.[54] Toward the end of her life, Osborn's entrepreneurial sister, Catherine H., an advocate of women's rights who never married and ran her own dry-goods businesses (in Wilmington, Delaware; Baltimore; Philadelphia; and Boston), also joined the family, living for a while in Iowa and then in Illinois with her brother Thomas C. until her death.[55] Only Osborn's oldest sister, Rachel, remained in Columbiana County, where she had married Elisha Dutton the year Philena's quilt was completed.

Major Life Changes

Philena's daughters, Angelina and Lorilla, were fourteen and eleven years old when Osborn gave up the mill in Forest Home and began devoting himself to the farm near Searsboro. Both girls attended primary and secondary school in the area while participating in the activities of the Lynn Grove Monthly Meeting along with the adults and socializing with their Searsboro neighbors, their friends in Forest Home, and the growing number of Osborn's relatives who arrived from Ohio over time. When the girls finished secondary school, Philena and Osborn sent them to Iowa College (now Grinnell College) to the north of Searsboro.[56]

Some of the early pioneers who settled in and around Forest Home were members of the Craver family. Osborn's sister Martha K. Hambleton had married Henry Craver in 1861, and it may have been through this aunt and uncle, or while she was attending Iowa College in Grinnell, that Angelina met Charles Francis Craver, Henry's cousin. Angelina and Charles were married on June 21, 1866, at her family's home in Searsboro.[57] Charles was twenty-three years old and Angelina was twenty-two.

Charles lived in Grinnell, a town twelve miles north of Searsboro named after the abolitionist Josiah Bushnell Grinnell. At the outbreak of the Civil War in 1861, Charles joined the Union forces. He enrolled at Grinnell as a private in Company E of the Fourth Iowa Volunteer Cavalry and was made a corporal in March of 1863. He reenlisted later in 1863 and by June of 1864 he had been appointed a sergeant major in the Fourth Iowa Cavalry. Charles's cavalry troop was the only one to go through the

ILLUSTRATION 50. Angelina Hambleton Craver (June 29, 1843–October 31, 1922) in the 1870s. Photo courtesy of the Jerome Walker family.

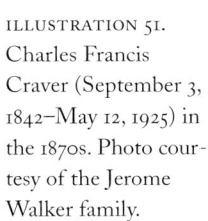

ILLUSTRATION 51. Charles Francis Craver (September 3, 1842–May 12, 1925) in the 1870s. Photo courtesy of the Jerome Walker family.

entire siege of Vicksburg, and a particularly interesting story of his war experiences was recounted in the May 19, 1925, edition of the *Grinnell Herald* after his death:

> One day in the spring of 1865 [a] squad of eight men [formed] a hollow square about a ninth [and] marched though the streets of Augusta, Ga. to the little port,

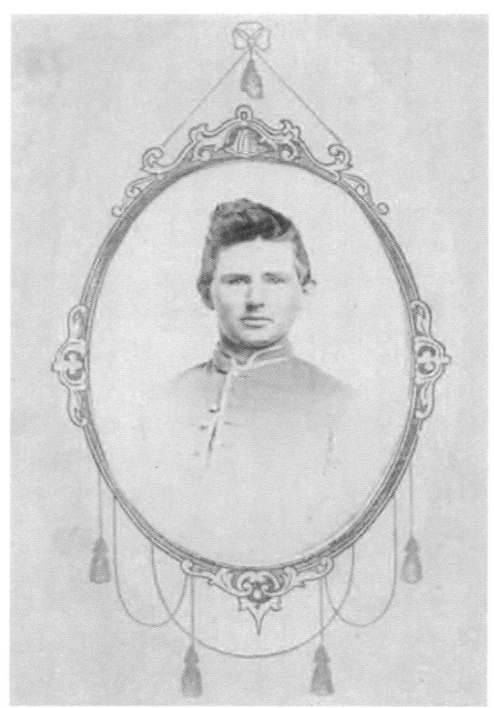

where a gunboat lay in wait for their arrival. Each man composing the square bore a cocked musket trained upon the solitary figure in the center, and had orders to shoot to kill at the slightest disturbance anywhere in the vicinity.

The ninth figure in the little group was Jefferson Davis, president of what was then the recent Confederate States of America. Craver was one of the eight Union soldiers delegated to guard the former chief executive during the march from the house where Davis had been under guard to the gunboat, which was to transport him away.

Charles was mustered out of the cavalry in Atlanta, Georgia, on August 10, 1865, and returned to Grinnell. After his marriage to Angelina the next year, he worked as a bookkeeper in a hardware store and later in the lumber business. In 1870, Angelina and Charles had their first son, Arthur Hambleton Craver. Two years later, the Craver home was destroyed by a cyclone that tore through Grinnell, and the family barely escaped to their underground cellar by running for their lives.

Charles served in the Iowa House of Representatives in the sixteenth Iowa General Assembly in 1876 and, in 1877, the Cravers had their second son, Frank Steele Craver. That same year, Charles formed a company with Alonzo Steele and J. M. Wells that manufactured farm equipment. The company, called Craver and Steele, was for many years the country's largest exporter of farming equipment—equipment that included the first successful twelve-foot "binder" for cutting and binding small grain, a machine that Charles himself had invented.[58]

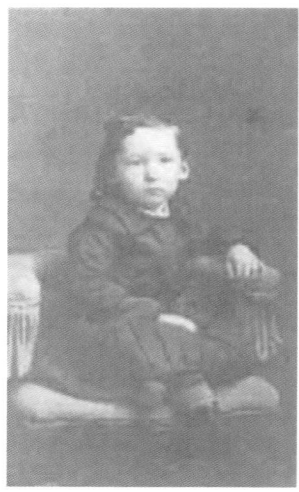

Philena and Osborn lived on at their property in Searsboro, content with his brother, her sister, and two daughters in the immediate area. In addition to the chores of farming, cooking, sewing, visiting their grandson, Arthur, and maintaining the family home, Philena most likely enjoyed a number of social events taking place in her community during this time. Typical of such events was the fiftieth wedding anniversary of neighbors Jarvis and Melissa L. Johnson—fellow members of the Religious Society of Friends and operators of a station on the Underground Railroad prior to the end of the Civil War. According to a newspaper account of this event that appeared in the Des Moines *Iowa State Register* on April 30, 1881, the celebration was held at the Johnson mansion near Lynnville, where guests were treated to a "most bountiful repast." There was a reading of the Johnson's marriage certificate followed by gift-giving. Joel and Phebe gave the couple a vase, a tidy (which was a piece of needlework placed on the arm or headrest of upholstered chairs to protect the fabric), and a one-dollar gold piece. Charles and Angelina Craver also attended, providing a bedspread and a flowering geranium. A Miss Hambleton, who was probably Lorilla, brought a bouquet, and Levi and Mary Hambleton were there from Oskaloosa to present a shawl pin and a two-and-a-half-dollar piece to the couple.

Philena and Osborn evidently did not attend this particular event even though seven members of their immediate family did. Their absence may have resulted from Osborn's declining health. He tragically passed away the next year on November 25, 1882. The cause of death was cited as "complications of Asthma."[59] Osborn was only sixty-four years old at the time and was taken to the Lynnville Friends Cemetery for burial. Here he joined his father, Benjamin, who had died in 1865 shortly after moving to Iowa from Ohio, his mother, Ann, who died two years later, and his little nephew, Thomas Fremont Hambleton, the son of Joel G. and Phebe, who was almost three years old when he died of diptheria in 1862.[60]

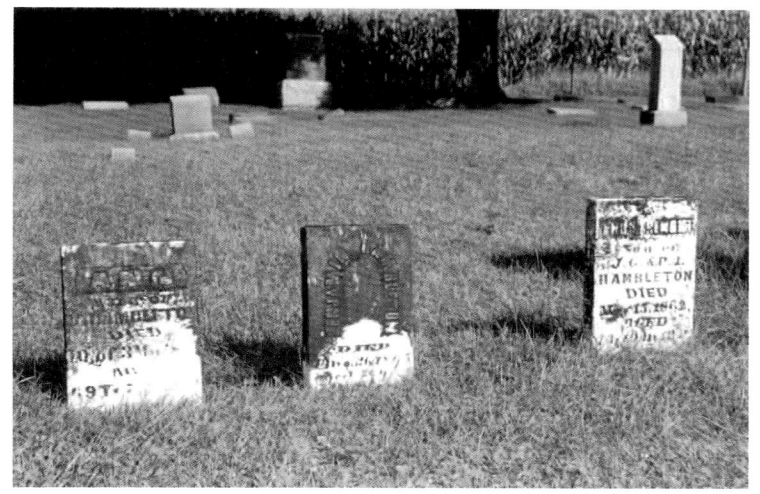

ILLUSTRATION 54. Lynnville Friends Cemetery. The tombstones are those of Ann Hanna Hambleton, Benjamin Hambleton, and Thomas Fremont Hambleton. Photo by Theodore Chenoweth, 2004.

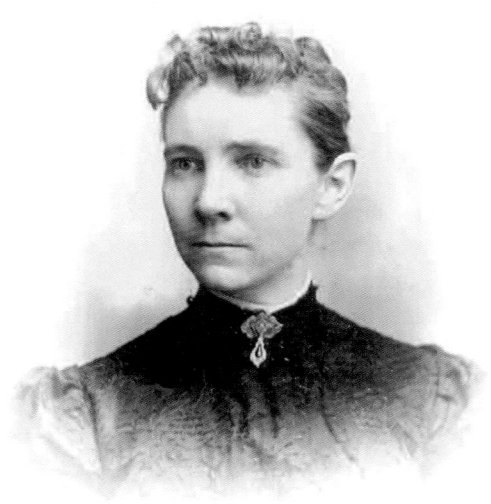

ILLUSTRATION 55. Lorilla Hambleton (April 20, 1847–December 6, 1914). Date unknown. Photo courtesy of the Jerome Walker family.

essary bedding (italics added), 2 beds, 150 pounds of meat, 10 bushels of potatoes, 3 dozen cans fruit, chairs and other furniture of value less than two hundred dollars, 2 tons of hay, and 5 hogs. The quilt Philena brought with her from Columbiana County may have been considered part of the "necessary bedding" she retained after Osborn's death.

Philena carried on after the death of her husband with the support of her sister and brother-in-law in Searsboro and her two daughters living close by in Grinnell. But in 1890 Charles and Angelina

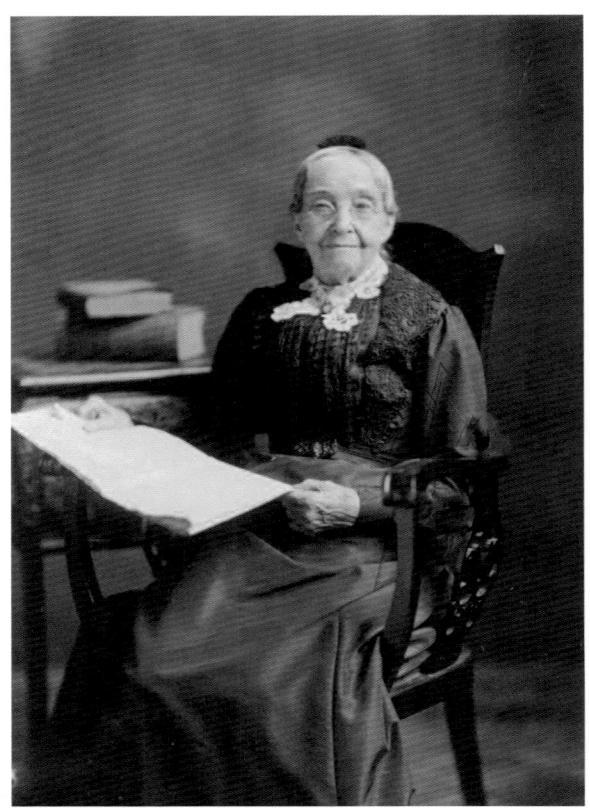

ILLUSTRATION 56. Philena Cooper Hambleton in Illinois, 1903. Photo courtesy of the Jerome Walker family.

Osborn's will, dated March 22, 1882, left all of his real and personal property to Philena and appointed her executrix of his estate. Her official estate inventory listed her two daughters as heirs. They were recorded as "A. C. Craver, daughter, 39, Grinnell, Iowa" and "L. A. Hambleton, daughter, 35, Grinnell, Iowa" indicating that, at the time of Osborn's death in Searsboro, Lorilla, who never married, was living with her sister in the Craver household.

The probate inventory also listed the following items that were to be retained by Philena as Osborn's widow: one horse, two cows, one single harness, one wagon, 25 bushels of corn, 2 bedsteads and *nec-*

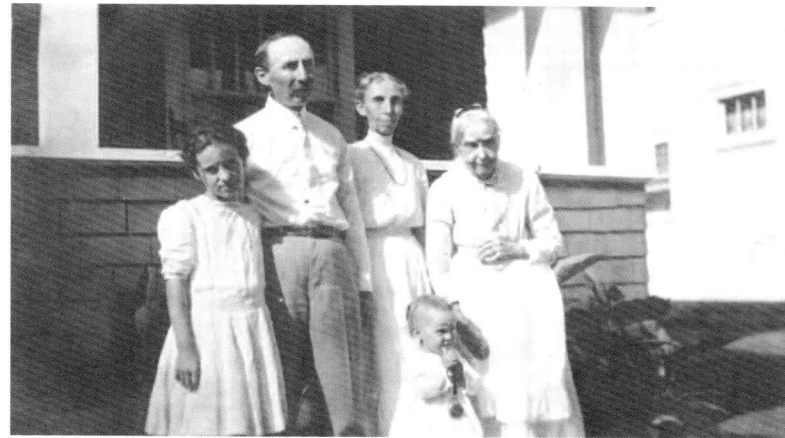

moved from Grinnell to Harvey, Illinois, just south of Chicago, where Charles felt his business, now called the Craver, Steele and Austin Manufacturing Company, would be better able to grow and prosper. Philena sold the Searsboro property in 1891[61] and, six years later in 1897, she was received, with Lorilla, in the Chicago Monthly Meeting—a Hicksite meeting in Cook County. From sometime in the 1890s until their deaths, both Philena and Lorilla lived with Charles and Angelina. When Charles and Angelina's son, Arthur, married his cousin Ada Mertilla Craver at the Cravers' Illinois home in 1901, both Philena and Lorilla were there to witness the event.[62]

The move to Harvey proved inopportune for Charles's company. The late 1890s produced a severe downturn in the economy, and Charles sought other endeavors, eventually in oil, which caused the Cravers, Lorilla, and Philena to move from Illinois to Oklahoma in 1907. Under the name Craver & Sons, Charles built a family oil business from Tulsa that extended over Oklahoma, Kansas, Louisiana, Texas, Arkansas, and Illinois.

Death in Oklahoma

Lorilla and Philena were living with the Cravers in Tulsa in 1912 when Philena's brother-in-law Joel G. passed away at Searsboro and was interred at the Lynnville Friends Cemetery. He was followed by Philena's daughter, Lorilla, who died on December 6, 1914. The *Grinnell Herald* reported on December 12 of that year that she had passed away in the Craver home in Tulsa and that her body had been brought to Grinnell before being taken to Lynnville for burial. Lorilla's death was followed one month later, on January 4, 1915, by that of Phebe, Philena's sister in Searsboro.[63]

The heartbreak of losing her youngest daughter and only sister within a single month must have been unbearable. On March 20, 1915, Philena also passed away in the Craver home. She was ninety-two years old. A notice of her death in the *Montezuma Weekly Republican* on April first stated that Charles Craver, his sister, and his brother-in-law accompanied her body back to Iowa. There was no mention of Angelina. Both Lorilla and Philena

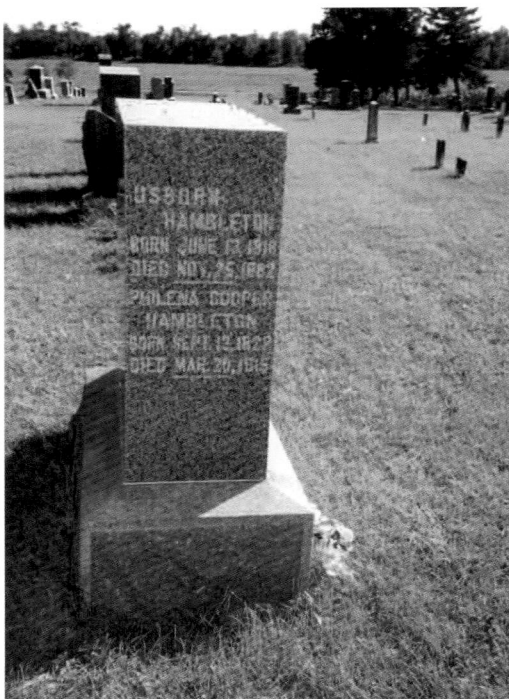 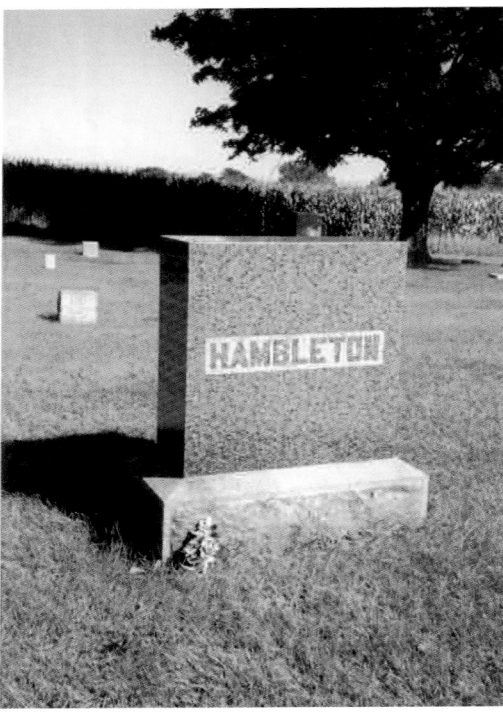

ILLUSTRATION 58. Lynnville Friends Cemetery in 2004. The marker that now rests over the graves of Osborn, Philena, and Lorilla Hambleton. Lorilla's inscription is on the other side of the marker. The author was unable to ascertain who erected this and two other modern Hambleton markers that designate the graves of Joel G. and Phebe Cooper Hambleton and that of their son Orlando, who died in 1902. Photos by Theodore Chenoweth, 2004.

were buried in the Lynnville Friends Cemetery next to Osborn.

When Philena passed away in 1915, she had out-lived at least thirty-one of the thirty-nine people whose names were inscribed on her quilt. The quilt bearing their names was with her for sixty-two years, serving as a testament to the lives of those she most cherished and as a comforting reminder of those she had known and loved in an earlier time.

With Philena's death, the quilt passed to her surviving daughter, Angelina. Angelina and Charles remained in Tulsa until their deaths. Both were active members of the Methodist Episcopal Church, and when Angelina died on October 31, 1922, to be followed by Charles on May 12, 1925, both were buried in Rose Hill Memorial Park in Tulsa, Oklahoma.

Instructions for Making a Replica of Philena's Quilt

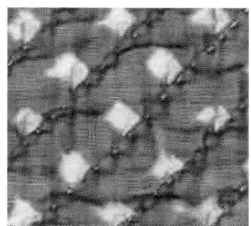

Please note that this is not a beginner project. Some quiltmaking experience is necessary. For more information about and instructions for fabric choice, rotary cutting, setting up your machine, pressing, cutting borders, assembling and basting the quilt "sandwich," quilting, and binding, please refer to one of the myriad fine books on the subject or take a class at your local fabric shop. Only the dimensions of the pieces and basic block- and quilt-top-construction directions are given here.

Pattern written by
Beth Donaldson

MATERIALS AND CUTTING

Block size 12" **Quilt Size** 82" x 82"

Requirements are based on 40" of fabric width

MATERIALS	YARDS	CUTTING
Cream	5	4 strips 6 ½" by 88" for borders. 25 A 200 B 32 F for sashing
Red Scraps	1 ¾ (9" x 20" per block)	100 D (4 per block) 100 C (8 per block)
Green	1 ¼ ¾	25 E For binding cut 2 ½" wide

Rotary Cutting

Measurements include ¼" seam allowances. Align arrows with lengthwise or crosswise grain of fabric.

Hints: Cut the strips for the borders first and set aside. The borders are cut long to allow for adjustments later. Cut and sew one quilt block, before cutting all pieces. Wait to cut the sashings and cornerstones until all blocks are sewn. This will allow you to make adjustments if you have problems as you complete your quilt.

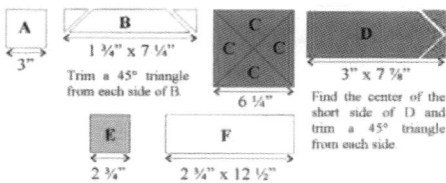

A — 3"

B — 1 ¾" x 7 ¼"
Trim a 45° triangle from each side of B.

C

D — 3" x 7 ⅞"
Find the center of the short side of D and trim a 45° triangle from each side.

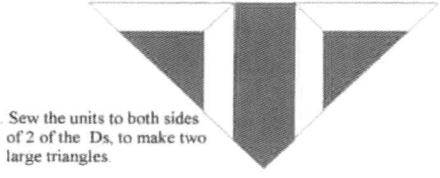

E — 2 ¾"

F — 2 ¾" x 12 ½"

6 ¼"

Assembling the Blocks

1. Sew one B to one C. Stop and backstitch ¼" from the corner of C.

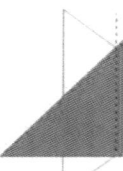

2. Sew one B to the other side of C. Stop and backstitch ¼" from the corner of C.

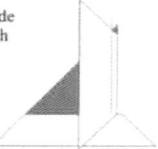

3. Sew the Bs together. Stop and backstitch ¼" from the corner of C.

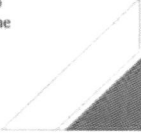

4. Repeat steps 1-3 to make a total of four triangle units.

5. Sew the units to both sides of 2 of the Ds, to make two large triangles.

6. Sew the remaining two Ds, to opposite sides of A.

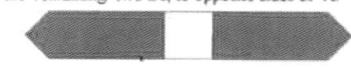

7. Layout all the units as shown, align edges and seams and sew the last two seams.

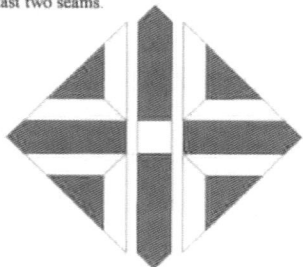

8. The block is finished and should measure 12 ½" x 12 ½".
   Sign the center square with a Pigma Pen (I like a thick #8).

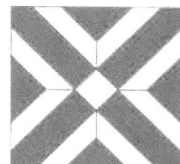

9. Make 24 more blocks.

Assembling the Quilt

10. Cut the Es and Fs. Lay them out in rows as shown. Sew the blocks and Fs to make 5 rows. Sew the Es and Fs to make 4 rows. Sew the rows together.

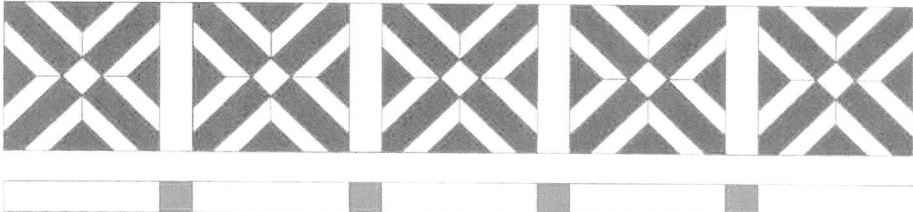

11. Use the strips set aside for the borders to cut the side borders 6 ½" x 69 ½". Sew them to the sides of the quilt top. Cut the remaining two strips 6 ½" x 81 ½". Sew them to the top and bottom of the quilt.

12. Layer the top, batting and backing and quilt according to the diagram. When the quilting is finished, bind off.

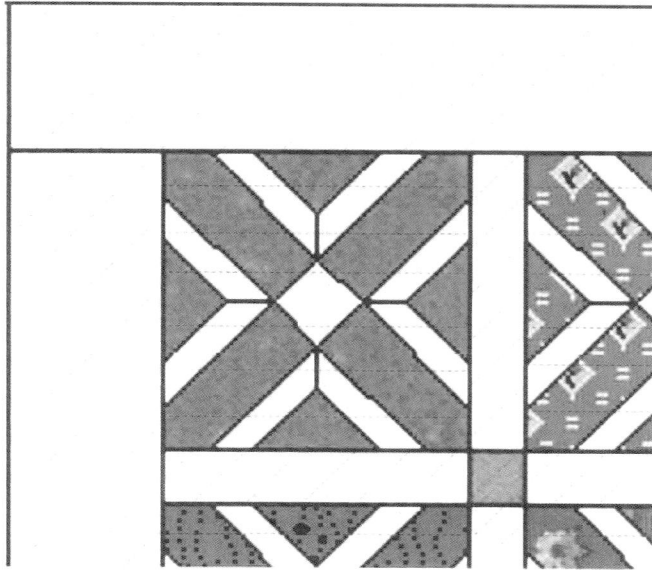

Notes

The quotation on the dedication page is from a letter by Anna Briggs Bentley published in *American Grit: A Woman's Letters from the Ohio Frontier,* ed. Emily Foster (Lexington: University Press of Kentucky, 2002), 67.

Signature Quilts

1. Barbara Brackman, "Signature Quilts, Nineteenth-Century Trends," in *Quiltmaking in America: Beyond the Myths,* ed. Laurel Horton (Nashville: Rutledge Hill Press, 1994), 20–29.

2. Linda Otto Lipsett, *Remember Me: Women and Their Friendship Quilts* (Lincolnwood, IL: Quilt Digest Press, 1985), 19–20, and Barbara Brackman, *Clues in the Calico: A Guide to Identifying and Dating Antique Quilts* (McLean, VA: EPM, 1989), 143–45.

3. Brackman, "Signature Quilts," 25.

4. Linda Eaton, *Quilts in a Material World: Selections from the Winterthur Collection* (New York: Abrams and The Henry Francis du Pont Winterthur Museum, 2007), 41.

5. The autograph album originated in the middle of the sixteenth century as the *album amicorum.* These albums were carried first by German students and scholars to collect the signatures of friends and associates as they moved from one university to another. For a history of these early autograph albums, see M. A. E. Nickson, *Early Autograph Albums in the British Museum* (London: Trustees of the British Museum, 1970).

Over time, it became a European tradition to collect the signatures of friends and family, as well as verses and drawings, in bound books or albums produced for this purpose. The tradition of collecting autographs appeared in America by the 1820s, and there exist several autograph albums dating from this period. To name a few, the Friends Historical Library of Swarthmore College lists among its Quaker "autograph books" (defined as "containing signatures of friends and acquaintances") an autograph album that belonged to Elizabeth M. Hewes dated 1827 (call number MSS002/59), one that belonged to Ann McIlvain dated 1825 (call number RG5/85), and another that belonged to Sarah L. Miller dated 1819 (also call number RG5/85). Another early example rests in the Library of the Winterthur Museum and Gardens. It is an autograph album, with sketches, that belonged to Eleuthera du Pont (part of Collection 710, du Pont family papers, accession number 65x623). Its entries span the period of 1824–58. The majority of the autographs were written in the 1820s by Eleuthera's family members and women friends, but the album also includes a notation with signature by the Marquis de Lafayette, penned during his American tour of 1824–25. For additional information about this album, consult the Library at Winterthur Museum or Lynn Ann Catanese, *Women's History: A Guide to Sources at Hagley Museum and Library* (Westport, CT: Greenwood Press, 1997), 121. The Lancaster County Historical Society Archives in Lancaster, Pennsylvania, contain an autograph album with entries dated 1827–32 that belonged to Elizabeth F. Allen (MG-118 Autograph Album Collection). A further example is the autograph album of Lucy Holmes Balderston in the manuscripts collection at the H. Furlong Baldwin Library of the Maryland Historical Society in Baltimore (MS 1796). This one includes entries dated 1824–48. The notations in the du Pont album, and those in the Balderston album, span thirty-four and twenty-four years, respectively, indicating that some women owned and continued to collect signatures in these albums well into adulthood.

6. Lipsett, *Remember Me,* 18–19. Additional sources of verse throughout the nineteenth century were "writers," a group of books containing verses suitable for use in autograph albums. Examples of the various types of verses

popular from the 1820s to the 1850s are provided by W. K. McNeil, "From Advice to Laments: New York Autograph Album Verse, 1820–1850," *New York Folklore Quarterly* 25, no. 3 (September 1969): 175–94.

7. Margaret T. Ordoñez, "Ink Damage on Nineteenth-Century Cotton Signature Quilts," in *Uncoverings 1992* (San Francisco: American Quilt Study Group, 1993), 148–68. According to Ordoñez, nineteenth-century inks made of carbon, known as India ink, were safe to use on fabrics, and several carbon inks were patented in the late 1830s and in the 1840s. Ink made using silver nitrate formulations was also considered safe. Other inks, however, such as iron gallotannate inks, continued to be used, and these have a history of causing fabric degradation on signature quilts. The fabric damage was caused by the acids in the ink that caused hydrolysis, a chemical reaction that occurred when these inks were applied to materials made from cellulose such as paper, linen, and cotton. For a history of the development of ink see David Carvalho, *Forty Centuries of Ink* (Charleston, SC: BiblioBazaar, 2006).

8. Sandi Fox, *For Purpose and Pleasure: Quilting Together in Nineteenth-Century America* (Nashville: Rutledge Hill Press, 1995), 27.

9. A number of terms have been used to describe signature quilt styles. The terminology used by Brackman ("Signature Quilts," 20–29) has been adopted for this publication.

10. Patsy and Myron Orlofsky, *Quilts in America* (New York: Abbeville Press, 1992), 249.

11. Brackman, "Signature Quilts," 20–29, and Schnuppe von Gwinner, *The History of the Patchwork Quilt: Origins, Traditions, and Symbols of a Textile Art* (West Chester, PA: Schiffer, 1988), 138.

12. Even though most documented signature quilts display the writing of several people, the inscription of quilts by a single hand was a common occurrence during the nineteenth century. Jane Bentley Kolter cites, in *Forget Me Not: A Gallery of Friendship and Album Quilts* (New York: Sterling, 1990), an appliquéd friendship quilt that was inscribed by a single hand and made in Chester County, Pennsylvania, in 1850 by Enzia Jackson (65). In her poignant book *Pieced from Ellen's Quilt: Ellen Spaulding Reed's Letters and Story* (Dayton, OH: Halstead and Meadows, 1991), Linda Otto Lipsett describes Ellen's marriage quilt as made up of

fifty-five blocks, "each inscribed with the appropriate name and town in beautiful old-style calligraphy by one person's hand" (19). In *Remember Me*, Lipsett discusses another quilt, this one made by Leonora Bagley, who pieced it herself and then had it inscribed by "someone with excellent penmanship and experience writing on cloth." She states, "When all blocks were to be signed by one hand . . . it was a common practice to baste a small strip of paper with the intended person's name to each block, so that no one would be accidentally omitted" (20–21). Jacqueline Marx Atkins, in her book *Shared Threads: Quilting Together—Past and Present* (New York: Museum of American Folk Art, 1994), notes while discussing signature quilts that "the signatures might not be the actual ones of the makers, for in many cases the person with the best penmanship was asked to sign all the names—whether or not that person had actually participated in the making of the quilt" (38). Barbara Brackman, in *Clues in the Calico,* also states, "Often a single individual with graceful penmanship inked the signatures on blocks made by different people" (146).

13. Kolter, *Forget Me Not,* 59.

14. Patricia T. Herr, "Quaker Quilts and Their Makers," in *Pieced by Mother: Symposium Papers,* ed. Jeannette Lasansky (Lewisburg, PA: Oral Traditions Project of the Union County Historical Society, 1988), 12–21.

15. Groups of Quaker signature quilts studied by Jessica F. Nicoll and The Heritage Quilt Project of New Jersey revealed a greater frequency of Quaker-made single-pattern friendship quilts than Quaker-made sampler album quilts. The frequency noted by the New Jersey project prompted speculation that the single-pattern friendship quilt style may have originated with Quaker quiltmakers. See Jessica F. Nicoll, *Quilted for Friends: Delaware Valley Signature Quilts, 1840—1855* (Winterthur, DE: The Henry Francis du Pont Winterthur Museum, 1986), 26, and Rachel Cochran, Rita Erickson, Natalie Hart, and Barbara Schaffer, *New Jersey Quilts 1777 to 1950: Contributions to an American Tradition* (Paducah, KY: American Quilter's Society, 1992), 94.

16. Nicoll, *Quilted for Friends,* 15. Nicoll's study of Quaker-made Delaware Valley quilts from 1840 to 1855 prompted this observation: "Quaker values manifested themselves in the quilts more symbolically than aestheti-

cally. The use of identical blocks [single-pattern blocks] not only gave the quilts a formal coherence, but presented an image of a unified community. On the quilts, whose purpose was to preserve the memory of specific people, individuality was not denied but was presented as an incremental part of a whole. Thus, the Quaker testimonies of equality and community were affirmed by those signature quilts which were composed, like the Quaker community, of discrete but equal units."

17. Errol T. Elliott, *Quakers on the American Frontier* (Elgin, IL: The Brethren Press, 1969), 70.

18. Ricky Clark, George W. Knepper, and Ellice Ronsheim, *Quilts in Community: Ohio's Traditions* (Nashville: Rutledge Hill Press, 1991), 132.

19. William Wade Hinshaw, *Encyclopedia of American Quaker Genealogy*, volume 4 (Ann Arbor: Edwards Brothers, 1946), 694, 932–33, 943; and One World Family Tree data under Judith Stanley at http://trees.ancestry.com/owt/person.aspx?pid=31873681, 4/5/2007.

20. The people named on Ann Coppock's quilt were identified by referencing census, marriage, and family tree information on the genealogical website http://ancestry.com; township property maps in the *Combined Atlas of Columbiana County 1841–1860* published by the Ohio Genealogical Society in 1983 and again in 1996; and family records contained in Hinshaw's *Encyclopedia of American Quaker Genealogy*, volume 4. Where possible, birth, death, and marriage information provided on http://ancestry.com family trees was confirmed by consulting Hinshaw. Only seven of the eighty-six people named on Ann's quilt could not be identified in this way.

21. The author's interpretation of the community depicted on Ann's quilt as one of youthful optimism and continuing friendship and support applies only to Ann's quilt and should not be construed to apply to bridal or marriage quilts in general. In fact, based on the gender, age, and relationship information Linda Otto Lipsett provided about the community represented on Ellen Spaulding Reed's bridal quilt (*Pieced from Ellen's Quilt*, 194–96), the same analysis produced a quite different impression, even though Ellen's quilt was made for the same purpose. The community on Ellen's quilt was generally more diverse and mature, even though Ellen was only one year older than Ann when she married. This may have been because Ellen's quilt was made by her married sister, Leonora Bagley, and included the names of many of Leonora's in-laws, friends, and neighbors. Also, Ellen's marriage involved leaving her community for a potentially dangerous and unpredictable future in the west, whereas Ann was continuing life as a married woman surrounded by her friends and relatives in the place where she grew up. The circumstances were different for these two women, and the communities represented on their quilts may, in part, reflect these differences.

22. Elliott, *Quakers on the American Frontier*, 60.

23. Ricky Clark, "Mid-19th-Century Album and Friendship Quilts, 1860–1920," in *Pieced by Mother: Symposium Papers*, ed. Jeannette Lasansky (Lewisburg, PA: Oral Traditions Project of the Union County Historical Society, 1988), 76–85.

Philena's Quilt

1. Eileen Jahnke Trestain, *Dating Fabrics: A Color Guide, 1800–1960* (Paducah, KY: American Quilter's Society, 1998), 44.

2. At the time Philena's quilt was made, Turkey-red fabrics were mainly imported from France and England. The process that produced them is thought to have originated in eastern India and then to have spread through Persia to Turkey centuries before. Turkey-red fabrics were exported to Europe in large quantities during the mid-seventeenth and into the eighteenth century from Constantinople—hence the name "Turkey" associated with their colorfast, vibrant red. These reds were not produced in America in commercially viable quantities until the introduction in 1869 of artificial alizarin, a dye derived from the successful synthesis of the coloring agent in madder root. Refer to Gösta Sandberg, *The Red Dyes: Cochineal, Madder, and Murex Purple* (Asheville, NC: Lark Books, 1997), 102; Joyce Storey, *The Thames and Hudson Manual of Dyes and Fabrics* (London: Thames and Hudson, 1978), 71; and, Diane L. Fagan Affleck, *Just New from the Mills: Printed Cottons in America* (Lowell, MA: American Textile History Museum, 1987), 55.

3. Brackman, *Clues in the Calico*, 63, and Trestain, *Dating Fabrics*, 42.

4. Brackman, *Clues in the Calico*, 63–64.

5. *The Discipline of the Society of Friends of Ohio Yearly Meeting; Printed by Direction of the Meeting, Held at Mount-pleasant, Ohio, in the Year 1819* (Mountpleasant, OH: Enoch Harris Jr., 1839), 90.

6. Mary Anne Caton, "The Aesthetics of Absence: Quaker Women's Plain Dress in the Delaware Valley, 1790–1900," in *Quaker Aesthetics: Reflections on a Quaker Ethic in American Design and Consumption,* ed. Emma Jones Lapsansky and Anne A. Verplanck (Philadelphia: University of Pennsylvania Press, 2003), 246–71.

7. Elisabeth McClellan, *Historic Dress in America, 1800–1870* (Philadelphia: George W. Jacobs, 1910), figures 259 and 262, and Joan Kendall, "The Significance of Styles of Dress within the Religious Society of Friends in England," in *August Edouart: A Quaker Album: American and English Duplicate Silhouettes, 1827–1845,* by Helen and Nel Laughon (Richmond, VA: Cheswick Press, 1987), xiii and xiv.

8. William Wistar Comfort, *Just Among Friends: The Quaker Way of Life* (New York: Macmillan, 1941), 68–69. Comfort notes that when it became evident by the turn of the twentieth century that Quaker dress now called attention to the wearer, Quakers ceased to wear distinguishing apparel and began dressing like the rest of the population. They still, however, avoided flashy colors and extreme styles.

9. Patricia J. Keller, *"Of the Best Sort but Plain": Quaker Quilts from the Delaware Valley, 1760–1890* (Chadds Ford, PA: Brandywine River Museum, 1996), 14–17.

10. Nicoll, *Quilted for Friends,* 14.

11. There are, for example, at least sixteen signed sampler album and single-pattern friendship quilts featuring reds from the period 1840–59, some made by Quakers, in Gloria Seaman Allen and Nancy Gibson Tuckhorn, *A Maryland Album: Quiltmaking Traditions, 1634–1934* (Nashville: Rutledge Hill Press, 1995), 14, 94, 98, 100, 103, 105, 107, 111, 113, 118, 121, 127, 129, 131, 144, 157.

Philena's Community of Family and Friends

1. Chalkley J. Hambleton, *Geneological [sic] Record of the Hambleton Family: Descendants of James Hambleton of Bucks County, Pennsylvania, Who Died in 1751* (Chicago: published for the author, 1887), 93.

2. The names and other information written on the quilt appear to have been inscribed by a single hand. Unfortunately, this cannot be demonstrated to the reader because the writing is too faint to be successfully photographed or scanned from the quilt. Also, the writing style appears to be Spencerian—a style of penmanship developed by Platt Rogers Spencer in the early nineteenth century. The style was widely introduced to the public in 1848 with Spencer's publication of the *Spencerian System of Practical Penmanship.* The Spencerian style for ladies was soon published in women's periodicals and instructional booklets that made the art of legible, flowing penmanship a skill easily acquired at home by middle-class women who had not had the benefit of formal schooling. For those who had, such as Quaker women, who were generally educated in rural primary schools or in Quaker schools, the Spencerian style would have been taught during its period of popularity from the early through the mid-nineteenth century. It bears noting that Catherine H. Hambleton, Philena's sister-in-law, was a schoolteacher and still present in the Hambleton home when Philena's quilt was inscribed. Refer to Sandi Fox, *For Purpose and Pleasure,* 29, and the preface to *The Theory of the Spencerian System of Practical Penmanship in Nine Easy Lessons* (Fenton, MI: Mott Media, 1985; originally published in 1874 by Ivison, Blakeman, Taylor, and Co.).

3. Henry Howe, *Historical Collections of Ohio: An Encyclopedia of the State,* volume 1 (Cincinnati: C. J. Krehbiel, 1907), 435.

4. Members of the Columbiana County Chapter of the Ohio Genealogical Society, *Combined Atlas of Columbiana County, Ohio 1841–1860* (Salem, OH: Columbiana County Chapter, Ohio Genealogical Society, 1984), 11–12.

5. "Minutes of the Proceedings of the New Garden Anti-Slavery Society, February 5, 1838 through July 31, 1840," Hanover Township Historical Society, Hanoverton, Ohio; Foster, *American Grit,* 156; and "Roll of Members of the Ohio Anti-Slavery Society, 1842–1865," James Barnaby Papers, Western Reserve Historical Society, Cleveland, Ohio.

6. Nicoll, *Quilted for Friends,* 15.

7. Clark, Knepper, and Ronsheim, *Quilts in Community,* 133.

8. Ibid., 132.

9. Eaton, *Quilts in a Material World,* 38.

10. Anne A. Verplanck, "Facing Philadelphia: Social Functions of Silhouettes, Miniatures, and Daguerreotypes, 1760–1860" (PhD diss., College of William and Mary, 1996), 91–92. It should be noted that photograph albums, both in the past and today, are often arranged in a similar manner.

Is the Quilt Really Philena's?

1. Hambleton, *Geneological Record,* 93.

2. Kolter, *Forget Me Not,* 60.

3. Philena's sister-in-law, listed on the quilt as Rachel Hambleton, married Elisha Dutton on April 7, 1853, and after that date would have been referred to as a Dutton. She had not yet married when the quilt was inscribed.

4. This information was taken from a variety of obituaries and "Iowa Pioneer" articles gathered by Pat Rowell from Poweshiek County newspapers, including the *Montezuma Republican,* the *Montezuma Democrat,* and the *Grinnell Herald.* Dates were not provided for all articles.

5. Hambleton, *Geneological Record,* 58.

6. The conclusion that the quilt made its way to California through members of the Craver family is based on information received in personal correspondence with Gary D. Craver of Centerville, Iowa, dated June 11, 2005, and on information provided by the Los Angeles family of Jerome B. Walker, Florence Philena Craver Oberholtzer's nephew, in July 2007. The information that the quilt was originally purchased from an estate sale in the East Bay, where Danville is located, was eventually provided by the dealer from whom the author purchased the quilt.

Philena's Story

Note: All referenced census data came from federal and state census records at http://ancestry.com and from *1850 U.S. Census, Columbiana County, Ohio,* volumes 1–3, ed. Dr. John F. Schunk (Wichita: S-K, no date).

1. Hambleton, *Geneological Record,* 57. Hambleton cites Philena's birth date as September 12, 1822. Her tombstone at the Friends Cemetery in Lynnville, Iowa, displays her date of birth as September 13, 1822. Philena's middle name was revealed in "Family History by Elva Tambling for Nellie Reynolds Cranker," March 16, 1921, Los Angeles, California

(courtesy of the Jerome Walker family). Nellie Reynolds Cranker was the daughter of Maria Louisa Clemson, Philena's half-sister. Elva Tambling was the granddaughter of Cecilia Hannah Clemson, another of Philena's half-sisters.

2. Hand-written account of the marriage of Calvin and Elizabeth Simcock Cooper from "Sadbury Monthly Meeting Marriages 1738–1830," Box PH-564, 124 and hand-recorded births from "Bradford Monthly Meeting: Births 1725–1884," Box PH-32, 4, Friends Historical Library of Swarthmore College. Whitson's birth date was recorded as May 27, 1792.

3. Information about the Erskine/Askey family was provided by direct descendant Michele DeParasis in personal correspondence during 2005. She had this to say about the Erskine/Askey name: "I believe that Captain Thomas Askey [an ancestor of Rachel's father] spelled his name as 'Erskine.' Several of his children used the name Erskine. (Say it out loud with a thick brogue—AIR-SKEEN.) This, according to family tradition, morphed to Askins and Askey."

4. "Bradford Monthly Meeting: Minutes 1816–1834," Box PH-34, 59, Friends Historical Library of Swarthmore College.

5. The account of Whitson teaching at Luthersburg was found in an article about the history of Clearfield County that appeared in the *Clearfield Progress* in July 1950 and was reproduced as part of the historic newspaper database at http://www.ancestry.com, 1/21/05. Rachel's birth date of September 6, 1804, is engraved on her tombstone at Grove Hill Cemetery, Hanoverton, Ohio. The date of their marriage was taken from "Family History by Elva Tambling for Nellie Reynolds Cranker."

6. The birth dates of the Cooper children were taken from "Family History by Elva Tambling for Nellie Reynolds Cranker."

7. This newspaper article was probably published in the *Montezuma Weekly Republican.* It was obtained from the Poweshiek County Historical Society in Montezuma, Iowa, and is, unfortunately, unattributed and undated. The fact that Whitson drowned and the date of the event came from "Family History by Elva Tambling for Nellie Reynolds Cranker." The 1850 census shows Whitson M. Cooper's birth place as Pennsylvania, so Whitson and Rachel were still living there at the time of Whitson's death. That being

the case, his logging accident probably occurred on the Susquehanna River.

8. The letter referenced here is in the possession of the Jerome Walker family.

9. Hinshaw, *Encyclopedia,* 4:819, cites 1833 as the year Phebe and Thomas V. Hall, with children Edwin, Rufus, William, Alfred, and Elizabeth, were issued a certificate to transfer from Cherry Street, Philadelphia, Monthly Meeting to the New Garden Monthly Meeting in Columbiana County. Prior to Cherry Street, Phebe and Thomas had been members of the Bradford Monthly Meeting in Chester County, Pennsylvania. One of Benjamin and Lydia Windle's children, Lydia Ann, was born in Ohio on October 5, 1834. Their prior child had been born in Chester County, Pennsylvania, in 1831. The birth dates of these two children were found at the "Pat's Families" Family Tree web site at http://awt.ancestry.com/cgi-bin/igm.cgi?op=GET&db=pat-95667&id=I025345, 1/19/2005. Their places of birth were taken from census data.

10. *Combined Atlas of Columbiana County,* 10, 30, and 38.

11. "Columbiana County, Ohio, Marriages, 1800–1870," 52, "Bradford Monthly Meeting: Births, 1725–1884," Box PH-32, 42 and "Bradford Monthly Meeting: Men's Minutes, Hicksite 1828–1880," Box PH-33, 98, Friends Historical Library of Swarthmore College, and Hinshaw, *Encyclopedia,* 4:690.

12. The map of West Township in 1841 from the *Combined Atlas of Columbiana County, Ohio* shows Thomas V. Hall's property clearly marked next to the town of Lynchburg. The 1860 map shows that his property had been sold to D. Reeder. Philena's quilt indicates the Halls were living in Iowa in 1853.

13. The birth dates of the Clemson daughters were taken from "Family History by Elva Tambling for Nellie Reynolds Cranker." This document also states that Cecilia had a twin who died at birth. "Gene Pool Individual Records—Births," at http://ancestry.com (full citation no longer available), 5/20/2002, showed another daughter, Lily, born in 1840. In any case, Lily was not shown as being in the household at the time of the 1850 census, nor was she named on Philena's quilt in 1853.

14. Anna's original letters are preserved as the Stabler Collection at the Maryland Historical Society and are published in *American Grit: A Woman's Letters from the Ohio Frontier,* ed. Emily Foster (Lexington: University Press of Kentucky, 2002).

15. According to W. W. Boyd ("Secondary Education in Ohio Previous to the Year 1840," *Ohio Archaeological and Historical Quarterly* 25, no. 1 [January 1916]: 118–34), there were only four secondary schools in Columbiana County prior to 1840: Salem Academy, founded in 1809; New Lisbon Academy, founded in 1814; Friends' School (Salem), founded in 1822; and Sandy Spring School, founded in 1839. The Sandy Spring School would have been the closest to Lynchburg, where Philena and Phebe lived after Rachel married Reuben Clemson. Philena was seventeen and Phebe was fifteen by the time this school was founded.

16. Hambleton, *Genealogical Record,* 57, and "Columbiana County, Ohio, Marriages, 1800–1870," 122.

17. Charles Elmer Rice, *A History of the Hanna Family: Being a Genealogy of the Descendants of Thomas Hanna and Elizabeth (Henderson) Hanna, Who Emigrated to American in 1763* (Damascus, OH: Aden Pim and Son, 1905), 18.

18. William C. Kashatus, *Just Over the Line: Chester County and the Underground Railroad* (West Chester, PA: Chester County Historical Society, 2002), 57, and Charles L. Blockson, *The Underground Railroad in Pennsylvania* (Jacksonville, FL: Flame International, 1981), 60.

19. Hambleton, *Genealogical Record,* 61–62.

20. Ibid., 57 and 65; also a summary of the history of the Sandy and Beaver Canal, http://www.geocities.com/Heartland/Prairie/6687/sandy.htm, 12/2/2004.

21. "Columbiana County, Ohio, Marriages, 1800–1870," 122. Hambleton cites the date of this marriage as June 1815.

22. Hinshaw, *Encyclopedia,* 4:820 and 870. New Garden Monthly Meeting records show that Benjamin, Ann, and their children Rachel, Osborn, Levi, Catherine H., and Joel G. were granted a certificate to transfer to the New Garden Monthly Meeting in Hanover Township from the Carmel Monthly Meeting on June 17, 1826, and were received on certificate five days later.

23. "Minutes of the Proceedings of the New Garden Anti-Slavery Society."

24. Hambleton, *Genealogical Record,* 57.

25. Columbiana County Recorder's Office Land Records, 17:512, Lisbon, Ohio. A "Conveyance of Water Rights" exe-

cuted in May 1830 deeded a portion of a stream owned by Samuel Grisell to Benjamin Hambleton "for the express purpose of conveying the water of the aforesaid stream into the mill belonging unto . . . Benjamin Hambleton."

26. *The History of Poweshiek County, Iowa* (Des Moines: Union Historical Company, Birdsall, Williams and Co., 1880), 42.

27. Hambleton, *Geneological Record,* 58. Angelina was probably named after Angelina Grimké**,** a noted abolitionist of the time.

28. Margaret L. Stuntz, *The Ancestors of Mahlon Votaw, 1826–1919,* volume 2 of the *Votaw Volumes* (Decorah, IA: Anundsen, 2001), 196.

29. The Ward, Windle, and Griffith families had several members. Only those named on Philena's quilt are mentioned here.

30. "Roll of Members of the Ohio Anti-Slavery Society, 1842–1865" and "Minutes of the Proceedings of the New Garden Anti-Slavery Society."

31. "Transcript of the Compromise of 1850" (including Clay's Resolutions and the First through Fifth Statutes), 1–14, provided at http://www.ourdocuments.gov, 5/26/2004.

32. H. D. Smalley, a biographical sketch of Stephen D. Mendenhall published in newspapers at the time of his death in 1893 and quoted by Thomas Corwin Mendenhall in "History, Correspondence and Pedigrees of the Mendenhalls of England, the United States and Africa" by William Mendenhall. Smalley states in describing Stephen Mendenhall: "He was one of the early Abolitionists of Eastern Ohio, and was earnestly and unselfishly devoted to the antislavery cause in which he was associated with such men as Parker Pillsbury, Marius Robinson, Charles Griffen and many others. He was uncompromising in his opposition to what he believed to be wrong and hestitated at no personal sacrifice in his devotion to duty. His home was a station on the 'underground railroad' and many a fleeing fugitive [*sic*] from the south received aid and comfort there and was helped along on his way to freedom in Queen Victoria's dominion in North America." Smalley's comments were found under Stephen D. Mendenhall on a Family Trees web page titled "My Mother's Mother's People" at http://www.ancestry.com/cgi-bin/igm.cgi?op=GET&db=wilsonmassey&id=I07640, 1/11/2005.

33. Henry Howe, *Historical Collections,* 438.

34. C. B. Galbreath, "Anti-Slavery Movement in Columbiana County," *Ohio Archaeological and Historical Quarterly* 30, no. 4 (October 1921): 355–95.

35. Dorothy Sterling, *Ahead of Her Time: Abby Kelley and the Politics of Antislavery* (New York: W. W. Norton, 1991), 213–14.

36. Howe, *Historical Collections,* 448, and Dale E. Shaffer, *Salem: A Quaker City History* (Charleston, SC: Arcadia, 2002), 30–50.

37. Foster, *American Grit,* 247–48. The "Dr. Peek" Anna refers to was actually David J. Peck, who was the first black person to receive a medical degree in America. Samuel Brooke was Anna's cousin, a leading abolitionist of the time and once editor of the *Anti-Slavery Bugle* in Salem, Ohio. The Cowles family singers were Giles Hooker Cowles, probably Betsey Mix Cowles, and one of her sisters. Betsey was an educational reformer, a Garrisonian abolitionist from Ashtabula County, and a friend of Stephen and Abby Kelley Foster. Information about Betsey Mix Cowles can be found in Linda Geary, *Balanced in the Wind: A Biography of Betsey Mix Cowles* (Lewisburg, PA: Bucknell University Press, 1989).

38. Hambleton, *Geneological Record,* 58.

39. *History of Poweshiek County, Iowa,* 679.

40. Thomas V. and Phebe Cooper Hall and their son and his wife, Alfred and Sarah Farrington Hall, are listed on Philena's quilt as being in Cedar County, Iowa, in 1853.

41. Foster, *American Grit,* 75.

42. N. Howe Parker, *Iowa As It Is in 1855: A Gazetteer for Citizens and a Hand-Book for Immigrants* (Chicago: Keen and Lee, 1855), 52.

43. Manaoh Hedge, *Past and Present of Mahaska County, Iowa* (Chicago: S. J. Clarke, 1906), 393, and *History of Poweshiek County, Iowa,* 386.

44. Information about Joel's and Phebe's move to Iowa was taken from an undated article from the *Montezuma Weekly Republican* titled "Joel Garretson Hambleton," Poweshiek County Historical and Genealogical Society, Montezuma, Iowa.

45. *History of Poweshiek County, Iowa,* 680.

46. "Joel Garretson Hambleton," article cited in note 44 above.

47. *Roses and Thorns of YesterYears, Searsboro, Iowa, 1876–1976* (no publisher, no date), 29 and 77.

48. An account of Joel's and Phebe's fiftieth wedding anniversary that appeared in the local Searsboro newspaper on March 30, 1901, described the large gathering of friends and family, and the many gifts the couple received. Ten years later they celebrated their sixtieth anniversary with a similar, though less formal, event during which many town residents and other friends paid calls to honor them.

49. Hedge, *Past and Present*, 393.

50. *Biographies and Portraits of the Progressive Men of Iowa: Leaders in Business, Politics and the Professions: Together with an Original and Authentic History of the State* (Des Moines: Conaway and Shaw, 1899), 554–55.

51. Mary Heston Hall Hambleton's obituary, *Montezuma Weekly Republican*, January 31, 1900.

52. Hambleton, *Geneological Record*, 59. At the time of the 1870 census, Henry and Martha K. were living on property adjacent to that owned by Joel G. and Phebe Hambleton, perhaps on a parcel purchased from them.

53. Columbiana County Recorder's Office Land Records, volume 70, 334–35, Lisbon, Ohio. The property sold for $2,400.00. In 2006 dollars, this sum equates to $37,946.

54. *Beasley's Oskaloosa Directory, 1876–77*, 50.

55. Hambleton, *Geneological Record*, 58, and undated, unattributed newspaper article about the Hambleton family at the Poweshiek County Historical and Genealogical Society, Montezuma, Iowa; probably from the *Montezuma Weekly Republican*.

56. "The Hambleton Family," *Montezuma Palladium*, date unknown.

57. Hambleton, *Geneological Record*, 58.

58. All information about Charles F. Craver was taken from obituaries and from genealogical information provided by Gary D. Craver of Centerville, Iowa. The cyclone incident is described in Hambleton, *Geneological Record*, 58.

59. Osborn's death is recorded in book 83, page 22, of the Poweshiek County Courthouse records stored in Montezuma, Iowa. Photocopies of his probate records were referenced at the Poweshiek County Historical and Genealogical Society in Montezuma.

60. The death dates for Benjamin Hambleton, Ann Hanna Hambleton, and Thomas Fremont Hambleton were taken from their tombstones in the Lynnville Friends Cemetery.

61. The date of sale, March 21, 1891, is recorded on the current deed to the property in the possession of Tassy Aldridge Guthrie in Searsboro, Iowa.

62. "Family History by Elva Tambling for Nellie Reynolds Cranker."

63. The death dates of Joel G., Lorilla, Phebe, and Philena were taken from their tombstones at the Lynnville Friends Cemetery.

Bibliography

Published Works

Affleck, Diane L. Fagan. *Just New from the Mills: Printed Cottons in America.* Lowell, MA: American Textile History Museum, 1987.

Allen, Gloria Seaman, and Nancy Gibson Tuckhorn. *A Maryland Album: Quiltmaking Traditions, 1634–1934.* Nashville: Rutledge Hill Press, 1995.

Atkins, Jacqueline Marx. *Shared Threads: Quilting Together—Past and Present.* New York: Museum of American Folk Art, 1994.

Beasley's Oskaloosa Directory, 1876–77. Oskaloosa: publisher unknown.

Biographies and Portraits of the Progressive Men of Iowa: Leaders in Business, Politics and the Professions: Together with an Original and Authentic History of the State. Des Moines: Conaway and Shaw, 1899.

Blockson, Charles L. *The Underground Railroad in Pennsylvania.* Jacksonville, FL: Flame International, 1981.

Boyd, W. W. "Secondary Education in Ohio Previous to the Year 1840." *Ohio Archaeological and Historical Quarterly* 25, no. 1 (January 1916): 118–34.

Brackman, Barbara. *Clues in the Calico: A Guide to Identifying and Dating Antique Quilts.* McLean, VA: EPM, 1989.

———. *Encyclopedia of Pieced Quilt Patterns.* Paducah, KY: American Quilter's Society, 1993.

———. "Signature Quilts, Nineteenth-Century Trends." In *Quiltmaking in America: Beyond the Myths,* edited by Laurel Horton, 20–29. Nashville: Rutledge Hill Press, 1994.

Carvalho, David. *Forty Centuries of Ink.* Charleston, SC: BiblioBazaar, 2006.

Catanese, Lynn Ann. *Women's History: A Guide to Sources at Hagley Museum and Library.* Westport, CT: Greenwood Press, 1997.

Caton, Mary Anne. "The Aesthetics of Absence: Quaker Women's Plain Dress in the Delaware Valley, 1790–1900." In *Quaker Aesthetics: Reflections on a Quaker Ethic in American Design and Consumption,* edited by Emma Jones Lapsansky and Anne A. Verplanck, 246–71. Philadelphia: University of Pennsylvania Press, 2003.

Clark, Ricky. "Making a Case for the Abolitionist Quilt." *Piecework* (July/August 1995): 66–70.

———. "Mid-19th-Century Album and Friendship Quilts, 1860–1920." In *Pieced by Mother: Symposium Papers,* edited by Jeannette Lasansky, 76–85. Lewisburg, PA: Oral Traditions Project of the Union County Historical Society, 1988.

Clark, Ricky, George W. Knepper, and Ellice Ronsheim. *Quilts in Community: Ohio's Traditions.* Nashville: Rutledge Hill Press, 1991.

Cochran, Rachel, Rita Erickson, Natalie Hart, and Barbara Schaffer. *New Jersey Quilts 1777 to 1950: Contributions to an American Tradition.* Paducah, KY: American Quilter's Society, 1992.

Columbiana County Chapter, Ohio Genealogical Society, Members of. *Columbiana County Ohio Cemetery Inscriptions.* Volumes 4, 5, and 12. Salem, OH: Columbiana County Chapter, Ohio Genealogical Society, 1978.

———. *Combined Atlas of Columbiana County, Ohio 1841–1860.* Salem, OH: Columbiana County Chapter, Ohio Genealogical Society, 1984.

Comfort, William Wistar. *Just Among Friends: The Quaker Way of Life.* New York: Macmillan, 1941.

The Discipline of the Society of Friends of Ohio Yearly Meeting; Printed by Direction of the Meeting Held at Mountpleasant, Ohio, in the Year 1819. Mountpleasant, OH: Enoch Harris Jr., 1839.

Eaton, Linda. *Quilts in a Material World: Selections from the Winterthur Collection.* New York: Abrams and

The Henry Francis du Pont Winterthur Museum, 2007.

Elliott, Errol T. *Quakers on the American Frontier.* Elgin, IL: The Brethren Press, 1969.

Foster, Emily, ed. *American Grit: A Woman's Letters from the Ohio Frontier.* Lexington: University Press of Kentucky, 2002.

Fox, Sandi. *For Purpose and Pleasure: Quilting Together in Nineteenth-Century America.* Nashville: Rutledge Hill Press, 1995.

Galbreath, C. B. "Anti-Slavery Movement in Columbiana County." *Ohio Archaeological and Historical Quarterly* 30, no. 4 (October 1921): 355–95.

Geary, Linda L. *Balanced in the Wind: A Biography of Betsey Mix Cowles.* Lewisburg, PA: Bucknell University Press, 1989.

Hambleton, Chalkley J. *Geneological [sic] Record of the Hambleton Family: Descendants of James Hambleton of Bucks County, Pennsylvania, Who Died in 1751 with Mention of Other Hambletons In England and America.* Chicago: published for the author, 1887.

Hedge, Manoah. *Past and Present of Mahaska County, Iowa.* Chicago: S. J. Clarke, 1906.

Herr, Patricia T. "Quaker Quilts and Their Makers." In *Pieced by Mother: Symposium Papers,* edited by Jeannette Lasansky, 13–21. Lewisburg, PA: Oral Traditions Project of the Union County Historical Society, 1988.

Hinshaw, William Wade. *Encyclopedia of American Quaker Genealogy.* Volume 4. Ann Arbor: Edwards Brothers, 1946.

History of Poweshiek County, Iowa. Des Moines: Union Historical Company, Birdsall, Williams and Co., 1880.

Howe, Henry. *Historical Collections of Ohio: An Encyclopedia of the State.* Cincinnati: C. J. Krehbiel, 1907.

Kashatus, William C. *Just Over the Line: Chester County and the Underground Railroad.* West Chester, PA: Chester County Historical Society, 2002.

Keller, Patricia J. *"Of the Best Sort but Plain": Quaker Quilts from the Delaware Valley, 1760–1890.* Chadds Ford, PA: Brandywine River Museum, 1996.

Kolter, Jane Bentley. *Forget Me Not: A Gallery of Friendship and Album Quilts.* New York: Sterling, 1990.

Lasansky, Jeannette, ed. *Pieced by Mother: Symposium Papers.* Lewisburg, PA: Oral Traditions Project of the Union County Historical Society, 1988.

Laughon, Helen, and Nel Laughon. *August Edouart: A Quaker Album: American and English Duplicate Silhouettes, 1827–1845.* Richmond, VA: Cheswick Press, 1987.

Lipsett, Linda Otto. *Pieced from Ellen's Quilt: Ellen Spaulding Reed's Letters and Story.* Dayton, OH: Halstead and Meadows, 1991.

———. *Remember Me: Women and Their Friendship Quilts.* Lincolnwood, IL: Quilt Digest Press, 1985.

McClellan, Elisabeth. *Historic Dress in America, 1800–1870.* Philadelphia: George W. Jacobs, 1910.

McNeil, W. K. "From Advice to Laments: New York Autograph Album Verse, 1820–1850." *New York Folklore Quarterly* 25, no. 3 (September 1969): 175–94.

Nickson, M. A. E. *Early Autograph Albums in the British Museum.* London: Trustees of the British Museum, 1970.

Nicoll, Jessica F. *Quilted for Friends: Delaware Valley Signature Quilts, 1840–1855.* Winterthur, DE: Henry Francis du Pont Winterthur Museum, 1986.

Ordoñez, Margaret T. "Ink Damage on Nineteenth-Century Cotton Signature Quilts." In *Uncoverings 1992,* 148–68. San Francisco: American Quilt Study Group, 1993.

Orlofsky, Patsy, and Myron Orlofsky. *Quilts in America.* New York: Abbeville Press, 1992.

Parker, N. Howe. *Iowa As It Is in 1855: A Gazetteer for Citizens and a Hand-Book for Immigrants.* Chicago: Keen and Lee, 1855.

Rice, Charles Elmer. *A History of the Hanna Family: Being a Genealogy of the Descendants of Thomas Hanna and Elizabeth (Henderson) Hanna, Who Emigrated to America in 1763.* Damascus, OH: Aden Pim and Son, 1905.

Roses and Thorns of YesterYears, Searsboro, Iowa, 1876–1976. No publisher, no date.

Sandberg, Gösta. *The Red Dyes: Cochineal, Madder, and Murex Purple.* Asheville, NC: Lark Books, 1997.

Schunk, John F., ed. *1850 U.S. Census, Columbiana County, Ohio.* Volumes 1–3. Wichita: S-K, no date.

Shaffer, Dale E. *Salem: A Quaker City History.* Charleston, SC: Arcadia, 2002.

Sterling, Dorothy. *Ahead of Her Time: Abby Kelley and the Politics of Antislavery.* New York: W. W. Norton, 1991.

Storey, Joyce. *The Thames and Hudson Manual of Dyes and Fabrics.* London: Thames and Hudson, 1978.

Stuntz, Margaret L. *The Ancestors of Mahlon Votaw, 1826–1919.* Volume 2 of the *Votaw Volumes.* Decorah, IA: Anundsen, 2001.

The Theory of the Spencerian System of Practical Penmanship in Nine Easy Lessons. Fenton, MI: Mott Media, 1985; originally published in 1874 by Ivison, Blakeman, Taylor and Co.

Trestain, Eileen Jahnke. *Dating Fabrics: A Color Guide, 1800–1960.* Paducah, KY: American Quilter's Society, 1998.

Verplanck, Anne A. "Facing Philadelphia: Social Functions of Silhouettes, Miniatures, and Daguerreotypes, 1760–1860." PhD diss., College of William and Mary, 1996.

von Gwinner, Schnuppe. *The History of the Patchwork Quilt: Origins, Traditions, and Symbols of a Textile Art.* West Chester, PA: Schiffer, 1988.

Unpublished Works

"Bradford Monthly Meeting: Births 1725–1884." Friends Historical Library of Swarthmore College.

"Bradford Monthly Meeting: Men's Minutes, Hicksite 1828–1880." Friends Historical Library of Swarthmore College.

"Bradford Monthly Meeting: Minutes 1816–1834." Friends Historical Library of Swarthmore College.

"Columbiana County, Ohio, Marriages 1800–1870." Salem Public Library, Salem, Ohio.

"Family History by Elva Tambling for Nellie Reynolds Cranker," March 16, 1921, Los Angeles, California. Jerome B. Walker family, Los Angeles.

Land Records. Columbiana County Recorder's Office, Lisbon, Ohio.

"Minutes of the Proceedings of the New Garden Anti-Slavery Society: February 3, 1838 through July 31, 1840." Hanover Township Historical Society, Hanoverton, Ohio.

Poweshiek County Court Records, Montezuma, Iowa.

Probate Records. Poweshiek County Historical and Genealogical Society, Montezuma, Iowa.

"Roll of Members of the Ohio Anti-Slavery Society, 1842–1865." James Barnaby Papers. The Western Reserve Historical Society, Cleveland, Ohio.

"Sadbury Monthly Meeting: Marriages 1738–1830." Friends Historical Library of Swarthmore College.

Archives

Columbiana County Chapter of the Ohio Genealogical Society Archives, Lisbon, Ohio.

Friends Historical Library of Swarthmore College, Swarthmore, Pennsylvania.

Hanover Township Historical Society, Hanoverton, Ohio.

Poweshiek County Historical and Genealogical Society, Montezuma, Iowa.

Salem Public Library, Salem, Ohio.

The Western Reserve Historical Society Library Archives, Cleveland, Ohio.

Index